The Spell of New Mexico

The Spell of New Mexico

TONY HILLERMAN, *Editor*

UNIVERSITY OF NEW MEXICO PRESS   *Albuquerque*

Library of Congress Cataloging in Publication Data

Main entry under title:

The Spell of New Mexico.

    1. New Mexico—Addresses, essays, lectures.
I. Hillerman, Tony.
F796.5.S64   978.9   76-21523
ISBN 0-8263-0420-6

CONTENTS

PREFACE

Pretentious as it sounds, and tough as it is to prove, there *does* seem to be something about New Mexico which not only attracts creative people but stimulates their creativity. Our state's status as a haven for visual artists is long and widely accepted. It's probably less well known that we are also home territory for more than a score of novelists and poets. In fact, I can list twenty-eight (with almost two hundred books to their credit) without overtaxing my memory—and I'm sure that overlooks a good many.

Given New Mexico's scanty population, that's a wildly disproportionate number of writers. What is it about New Mexico, then, that seems to turn the imagination fertile? Jack Rittenhouse and I had wasted idle moments for years speculating on that question. Finally it occurred to us to go directly to the source. Why not allow the writers and artists to provide their own answers in their own words?

Rittenhouse (an editor at the University of New Mexico Press and my nominee for New Mexico's most erudite citizen) was already familiar with many of the sources. Since he was also willing to do most of the work, why not indeed?

The first step was to limit the target. This book would not be an assortment of physical descriptions. Instead it would focus on the effect of this state of ours upon the mind. It would be generally introspective, the words of people considering the impact of their environment upon their spirit, or their work. Since it would be about stimulation, we would rule out those in whom New Mexico produced only negative vibrations. They tended, after all, to be the sort for whom no genuine New Mexican would feel any fondness.

For example, among the excluded:

Secretary of War Charles M. Conrad, who suggested in 1852 that the United States should buy back what little property was in private ownership and give the entire territory back to the Indians.

General William Tecumseh Sherman, who in 1864 recommended to the House Military Affairs Committee that a diplomatic effort be launched to "prevail upon Mexico to take it back."

Edith M. Nicholl, who in her 1898 *Observations of a Ranchwoman in New Mexico* reported our population was "unsupported by intelligence" and called our landscape "a vast solitary waste."

There are others of similar dreary turn, such as James W. Gleed, who detected in us "an utter lack of beauty, the startling and omnipresent ugliness of both men and women," and the *New York Times* editorialist who wrote in 1871 that Santa Fe was "the heart of our worst civilization."

Unfortunately, these guidelines also pretty well eliminated New Mexico's native sons and daughters. While some of them wrote about New Mexico, none of them had much to say in print about its effect upon them. This awareness seems to come only upon return from exile, as with Harvey Fergusson, or to immigrants. Those born to the "spell of New Mexico" seemed, naturally enough, to take it for granted.

The material which follows is presented as originally published. Time, thus, has made some of the remarks anachronistic. For example, the scarcity of Albuquerque streetcars upon which Ernie Pyle comments has long since become absolute. But anachronisms aside, the light these essays cast on how New Mexico stimulates the imagination hasn't dimmed.

Tony Hillerman

Introduction

TONY HILLERMAN

*Tony Hillerman, professor of journalism at the University of New
Mexico, has published seven books of fiction and nonfiction. His* Dance
Hall of the Dead, *set at Zuni Pueblo, won the Edgar Allan Poe award of
the Mystery Writers of America as the best suspense novel of 1973.*

Of the persons whose words are included in this book I was
personally acquainted with only two. Oliver La Farge and
Winfield Townley Scott were both Santa Feans at the time I was
editing the *New Mexican,* Santa Fe's newspaper. For ten dollars a
week, La Farge wrote a witty, urbane column about the community's manners and morals. Also for ten dollars per week (which
he used to pay for reviews) Scott served as book editor. I have
since come to be ashamed of this brazen exploitation of their
sense of civic responsibility, but the association gave me a chance
to understand what held these two remarkable men in a climate and landscape so foreign to their native New England. Significantly, the things that appealed to them were almost totally
different.

La Farge, as much as any man I have ever known, was tuned to
people. His sensitive antennae were always fully extended to the
fellow humans around him. La Farge treasured New Mexico
because it offered—probably more than any place in America—a
rich variety of human cultures, religions, and value systems, and
because it attracted and held an interesting variety of immigrants.
If La Farge appreciated the landscape it was because of its effect

on the human spirit. La Farge was, first and always, a humanist in the basic sense of that word. But for Scott, as he says himself on one of the following pages, the magic lay "in the land itself."

"The breadth and height of the land, its huge self and its huge sky, strike you like a blow," Scott wrote in his "Calendar of Santa Fe." He described the cranky old city and its setting in terms of adobe walls, the red reflection of its sunsets, its sounds, smells, and winter silences. La Farge, on the other hand, explained the attraction of Santa Fe (in an article for the *New Yorker*) in terms of three Sisters of Loretto shoveling sand into the back seat of a Chrysler.

For La Farge it was always the people, the culture, the values, the patterns of human thought and human behavior. He made Laughing Boy one of the great living, breathing characters of American fiction—but the Navajo Reservation, on which Laughing Boy lived, was "an ash heap of desert."

Scott, like the Navajos themselves, saw the harsh and powerful grandeur of the land within the Sacred Mountains, the gradations of colors, the tortured, eroded shapes, the infinite variety of desolate beauty. But you'll find Scott generalizing that middle-aged Indians are "stout and appear nonvirile and nonsexual." La Farge saw in them the fascinating, mind-boggling variety of the human personality.

From this one might conclude that poets such as Scott love New Mexico for its landscape, and that the humanists, like La Farge, love it for the people it produced and the people, like Scott, it attracted. But it's not that simple.

My own experience lies somewhere between—but much closer to Scott than to La Farge. Writing (or at least writing tolerably well) is difficult for me. It requires intense concentration and it's helped by a particular mood. That's true of several other writers I know, and I suspect it's also true of almost everyone engaged in forcing the reluctant imagination to produce.

New Mexico is rich in locales where this mood, this excitement, this urge to write seems to come. Those places that stir me have features in common. All are empty and lonely. They invoke a sense of both space and strangeness, and all have about them a sort of fierce inhospitality.

One such place is east of U.S. 54 near the old Three Rivers service station north of Tularosa. The road jolts across the Southern Pacific tracks toward the foothills of the Sierra Blanca and passes a high, grassy ridge. On a July afternoon, the view from there suggests a hostile planet. The ragged stone ridgeline of the Sierra Oscura rises fifty miles to the west, and the Tularosa Basin below is lost in a haze of heat. If you climb high enough and the light is right, you can see to the southwest the glittering line formed by the gypsum dunes of White Sands and below the Oscuras the black smudge of the lava-bed badlands.

For me, this is one of many of New Mexico's magic places. And the magic seems always to have worked. Stone Age hunters used this same ridge before the white man arrived. They used it, I presume, because it commanded game trails. But while they waited, they covered the boulders with petroglyphs of beasts, men, and myth. Some of them suggest Miró, or Klee, or Picasso. All of them suggest that sitting among these basalt boulders, with no sound but the wind blowing through the gramma, and the arid immensity of the Tularosa Basin around you, stimulated imaginations which predate my own.

I could list a dozen such places—the lava flow that stretches south from Interstate 40 east of Grants; the Bosque del Apache on winter mornings when the snow geese are flying and the sky is full of the sound of birds; the ruined, eroded one-time grazing country that stretches south of Shiprock; the cold ridge on which the village of Truchas is built; and the eastern plains, which inspired in Conrad Richter the concept of his classic *The Sea of Grass.* I have never yet made that long, monotonous drive through the great vacancy between Albuquerque and Roswell without finding my head filling with ideas crying to be written.

One of our Pueblo peoples has, as a part of their emergence myth, a story that applies. When these people emerged from the underworld, they found the earth dark and empty. They saw only a giant sitting beside a fire. The giant was Skeleton Man (he has many other names), the Holy Person in charge of death. Skeleton Man's face was bloody and terrible, but his manner was friendly. The delegation asked if he had any objections to their living in his territory.

"No," said Skeleton Man. Immigrants were welcome. In fact, he would be glad to have neighbors, but they should understand that this land offered little food and less water. If they sought material benefit, they should seek elsewhere. They should remain only if fulfillment for them required things other than wealth and plenty.

The culture of the Pueblo Indians rates material goods low on the scale of life's values. They opted to stay. So did the Navajos, who have their own legend of how the Hero Twins decided not to kill Hunger when they were wiping out the monsters that infested Dinetah. They decided Hunger should share the land because the Navajos should not, in effect, live by bread alone.

For New Mexico, Skeleton Man's forecast of the economic prospects has been emphatically confirmed by per capita income statistics of the Department of Commerce. By any material standards, ours is a poor state, and it looks poor. Its eternal drought, its barrenness, its immense and sterile badlands show at a glance. Except for a few narrow river valleys, it offers none of those views of lush, green fertility that speak to the primal subconscious of food, comfort, security, wealth, and, therefore, of beauty. It's obvious that New Mexico didn't attract migrants with any glittering promises of easy living. Its appeal was to those—like the delegation calling upon Skeleton Man—who had values a little different from the materialism of American society.

Probably there's more to this "spell of New Mexico" than any of this. Probably it's almost purely individual. D. H. Lawrence, for example, wrote that New Mexico made him aware of "the terrifying underdepths" that lie beneath civilized society and thereby changed him forever. "Curious as it may sound," he wrote, "it was New Mexico that liberated me from the present era of civilization."

As for me, I can only say that New Mexico seems to make me want to write.

The Land of Journeys' Ending

MARY AUSTIN

Mary Austin (1868–1934)—playwright, poet, essayist, and novelist—produced some thirty-five books and hundreds of shorter works in a career that spanned forty-two years and stretched from California to New York to Santa Fe.

There can be no adequate discussion of a country, any more than there can be of a woman, which leaves out this inexplicable effect produced by it on the people who live there. To say that the Southwest has had a significant past, and will have a magnificent future, because it is a superb wealth-breeder, is to miss the fact that several generations of men wasted themselves upon it happily, without taking any measure of its vast material resources. The nineteenth-century assault, which found California a lady of comparatively easy virtue, quailed before the austere virginity of Arizona; but the better men among them served her without recompense. If the Southwest is becoming known as an unrivaled food-producer, still, food-producing is one of the things man has taught the land to do since he has lived in it. There was nothing that betrayed its crop capacity to the untutored sense of the Amerind savage and the unlettered American pioneer. Both of these married the land because they loved it, and afterward made it bear. If more lines of natural development converged here, between the bracketing rivers, more streams of human energy came to rest than anywhere else within what is now the United States, it was because men felt here the nameless content of the creative spirit in the presence of its proper instrument.

Such a country as this, calls its own from the four world quarters. It had called many known and some forgotten peoples before any European, just to hear of it, had been afoot, in that neighborhood, and that not of his own wish, for seven years.

New Mexico

OLIVER LA FARGE

A prolific writer who won the Pulitzer Prize for his 1929 novel Laughing Boy, *Oliver La Farge (1901–63) was also an eminent anthropologist and activist for Indian rights.*

Not so long ago a merchant in the town of Española, New Mexico—which lies some twenty-five miles north of Santa Fe at the junction of U.S. Routes 64, 84, and 285—requested an Eastern manufacturer for an estimate on a sizable order of his product. The manufacturer sent back an estimate in pesos, with instructions as to the type of international bank draft he would require. The Española man had a lot of fun answering that letter.

A New Mexican never ceases to be surprised to hear visitors —standing within sight of a Chevron filling station, a clearly labeled United States post office, and a Coke-advertising drugstore, with a movie theater right down the street—ask the tariff on a purchase they are contemplating "when we take it back to the States." Often the tourists are distinctly sorry to be disillusioned, and offer considerable resistance.

Nevertheless, New Mexico belongs to the United States family, species *Western,* subspecies *Southwestern;* it's un-American only in its thoroughly American insistence on being its own kind of place. If you ask a New Mexican what constitutes the Southwest, he will name New Mexico and Arizona; after hesitation, he may add the adjacent portions of Colorado, Utah, and Nevada. California, Texas, and Oklahoma he rejects, for reasons which will appear later.

The state partakes of the nature of all its species. It is large, the fifth largest in the Union, 122,634 square miles—but we don't think of ourselves as being so big, it's just that so many of the other states are smaller. The population is increasing fairly rapidly, but by Eastern standards it remains sparse. Its lowest portion, in the southeast, dips below 3,000 feet—which to a New Mexican is virtually sea level—is intolerably hot in summer, and achieves subtropical flora and fauna where there is sufficient moisture. In the north, its mountains climb high; two of its highest peaks, Truchas and Wheeler, reach above 13,000 feet. There we have ski runs, and at the highest levels you might encounter even white ptarmigan, if you are very lucky and your lungs hold out.

Between those extremes the variety is great. You can be camping up in the northern mountains, and in the morning break up your camp under blue spruce and fir, wrangling your horses out of the lush grass and the columbines in the meadow where you caught your breakfast trout. By noon you can take your break under cottonwoods in an irrigated section of orchards and corn and chili fields, and camp that night in desert where you are lucky, and distinctly relieved, when you find a water hole. You could, alternatively, stay in the mountains until the heavy winter snows close you in.

The state has flat, drab, repulsive, strangely fascinating desert by the mile, dramatic, colorful canyon country, and vast spaces of open, sparse, yet productive range land. It has little Spanish villages of adobe houses, as close-clustered as medieval towns around their miniature plazas and churches.

You can fish for trout in clear streams and mountain lakes, and you can camp by arroyos which, if you dig down a few feet under their dry sands, may or may not yield up that seep of water which will sustain life—and down which the roaring waters of a cloudburst that happened fifty miles away can come at sixty miles an hour in a wall ten feet high, with a haze of dust hovering over the rushing wall and whole trees revolving in its mass.

We have certain conventional expectations of beauty, in

mountains, in combinations of green land and water, in gaily painted cliffs or bright desert, but the perceptive eye learns to see beauty in less obvious forms. Much of New Mexico's real estate seems barren and monotonous on first sight; with a little time, as with the sea, those who live with it before their eyes learn to follow the constantly shifting moods, the delicate and incessant changes of light from day to day and from hour to hour, which give that empty-seeming country a life of its own.

Like most Western states, to a usually beautiful landscape New Mexico adds qualities of spaciousness, grandeur, and drama. It also achieves softness. Its mountains, very old, lying at the southern end of the chain of the Rockies, do not rise to the line of eternal snow; relatively few peaks reach above timber line. They are not jagged but worn round by aeons of time. One might say that, like so much in this new-old state, they are older and mellower than the mountains of its neighbors.

Most Western states have, and exploit, Indians. New Mexico, next to Arizona, has by far the largest proportion of full bloods and of Indians living a basically Indian life. The presence of this picturesque element is one of the reasons why it is a great tourist state, to the profit of the Indians and of the community as a whole.

The Indians can be listed among the state's natural resources. Others are oil, gas, potash, pumice, and a scattering of other metals and minerals, to the list of which vanadium is the latest addition. These assets, and the lumber of its forests, have made wealth here and there, but they are not enough to make New Mexico rich. It is a ranching state, with cattle predominant in the center, south, and east, sheep more to the north and west. Although your self-respecting cowpuncher still hates a lamb, the old, deadly sheep-and-cattle wars are over; the choice of which to run on a given range is made according to the nature of the feed and the terrain.

The average visitor, who wonders how animals can live on its sparse grazing lands, finds it hard to believe that New Mexico is also agricultural. Where there is water, it is.

Where there is water—that's the point. So seldom is there water, never is there enough water. In the richest parts of the mountains rainfall reaches thirty inches a year, but along the Rio

Grande Valley the *average* is ten inches, which means that one dry year means hardship, several dry years in succession mean privation and ruin for men, crops, and beasts. Of those few inches, much falls in storms so violent, in such masses, that the ground cannot absorb it and it runs off in flash floods. The dryest, most desert country is seamed, scarred, and excavated by the violence of floodwaters. These waters are caught in the main rivers, but bring with them tons of silt, raising the river beds, so that another paradox of this hard land is the loss of tons of water and miles of good land through the development of marshes.

The life of the state, of the crops, of the grass which feeds the cattle and sheep, depends upon the winter snows and the chancy advent of gentle rains, what the Indians call she-rains, in July. A good snowfall in the highlands means steady water in the little creeks, which means in turn a flow in the irrigation ditches all through the growing season. Then the ribbons of fertile land above the watercourses will be richly green, there will be corn, wheat, apples, apricots, and alfalfa, the horses will be sleek, and in the fall fat lambs and calves will go to market and the drying strings of chili will make masses of scarlet against the warm brown walls of the adobe farmhouses.

Water is life, and the theft of water may be punished, extralegally, as one would punish the taking of life—which is one of the reasons why men are meticulous about closing their water gates the moment their time for irrigation is up. The last fight I know of occurred in one of the mountain villages in the dark. Epifanio Tal, as we may call him (the case did not come to court, so I don't want to use real names), had the water from midnight till two, Amadeo Fulano got it at two. Their watches did not agree. Epifanio still had the water running on his place when Amadeo went to open his gate, so he came storming across the field with his lantern in his hand. Both men were irritable from lack of sleep. Finally, Amadeo reached to turn off his neighbor's water, and Epifanio poked him in the stomach with his hoe handle, knocking him down. Epifanio picked up a stone and threw it, knocking Amadeo out cold. No one was seriously hurt and, both men being devout members of the cult known as *Penitentes*, the Elder Brother who was head of that order in their village stepped in and got them to patch up their quarrel.

10

Men may take the law in their own hands; there is also a special body of law dealing with water. As English common law never embraced irrigation, this body is based upon the ancient water laws of Spain.

The importance of water is personified in the famous Rio Grande. Take a look at it; it is a poor-seeming body of water, often no more than a muddy trickle, sometimes only a dry river bed, hardly worthy, anyone would say, of its high-sounding name or its place in the American mind. This meager stream is the subject of interstate disputes, of hearings in Congress, the occupation of special boards and committees. It is the subject of compacts between states and of treaties between the United States and Mexico; the construction of a dam near its headwaters may be a subject of international concern. The prosperity or reversion to desert of thousands of miles of land in both republics, from Colorado to the Gulf of Mexico, depends upon the vagaries of this unpromising-looking stream, and upon man's use and abuse of it and its tributaries.

The volume of water that moves in it is, in fact, considerable, but at every point along its length most of the constant flow is drawn off into the ditches, which is why it, and many other New Mexico rivers, seem so pitifully inadequate. The water may be flowing miles from the river bed, used to the last drop, and even so there is never enough.

In an acute form, then, New Mexico has the Western characteristic of too little water, which is one of the standard Western gripes. Another is that it is economically a colony, a producer of raw materials, much of the profits from which, including a considerable part of the profits of the cattle industry, are siphoned off to the East and West Coasts. The ultimate development of the state is to an alarming degree dependent upon the decisions of people to whom it is not home, is not essential, but merely an investment to be held only so long as it yields a good return.

In all of these things I have been describing a typical Western state with a few local peculiarities; New Mexico differs from all of her forty-nine sisters in far more than those. We are, for instance, a state which has the East on both sides of it, and much of the West to the east of it. The presence of California on the other side, with only our close sister, Arizona, between, is what puts us in the position of having the East on both sides; for Californians, in outlook, speech, habits, and in their less effulgent forms of raiment, are definitely Easterners. They form one of the two largest bodies of our tourists, and on the whole they are intelligent, appreciative visitors, even though it must be admitted that they do drive like madmen.

As to a large part of the West being to the east of us, I have reference to the sovereign (and don't forget it) state of Texas, and what seems to be its colony, Oklahoma. Texas claims above all to be The West, yet a New Mexican thinks of a Texan as being from, if not of, the East, and a New Mexican, Indian or non-Indian, will automatically speak of members of such Oklahoma tribes as Kiowas, Cheyennes, or Osages as "eastern Indians."

Texas bulks large in our consciousness. For years, being a claiming sort of state, it claimed half of New Mexico, clear to the Rio Grande. It once even launched an invasion to annex the area. Latterly, the Texas have gone in for more peaceful conquest. Towards the Mexican border, in the area of the big cattle ranches, a large portion of the population derives from our neighbor to the south, while the eastern part of New Mexico, where it marches with the Lone Star State, is known as "the Texas Strip," because of the Texan dominance.

New Mexicans look down upon their great neighbor. Why shouldn't they? If they looked levelly towards the east, all they would see is sky. Any New Mexican can, and if given the opportunity will, tell you that New Mexico could be bigger than Texas if she chose to spread herself thin and flat, as her neighbor does. Texans, who comprise the other principal group of our tourists, condescend right back at us with vigor and often with charm.

An amiable sort of running feud goes on between the people of the two states, keeping both on their toes. When a Texan told me one time that he was a *real* old-timer, and that he personally had dug out the bed of the Pecos River, the Lord gave it to me to answer that, while he was doing that, I was up in the Sangre de Cristos melting snow to run in his ditch.

This exchange left us both happy and led to an agreeable acquaintance.

The Texan settlers form one of the elements in the endless

diversity that is New Mexico. If they give the tone to the east and south, the north and west are colored and dominated by the Spanish-Americans.

The ancestors of these Spanish-Americans settled this country before Virginia or the Bay Colony existed, and have lived here ever since. They have been citizens of the United States for over a century, fought in the Civil War and in every major war since; they are devotedly patriotic, and as a regular thing send more than their share of men into the nation's battles.

New Mexico is the one place where the question of the hyphen is approached logically, although the logic leads to a beautiful illogic. All Americans except Indians are considered hyphenated; we are divided into two groups, Spanish-Americans and Anglo-Americans, and, just as in Salt Lake City even Jews are Gentiles, so here all but the Spanish are Anglo-American regardless of national origins.

One of the leading "Anglos" of Santa Fe is Chinese. About fifty years ago the *New Mexican,* the Santa Fe paper, mentioned that "a Chinaman" had arrived in town to open a laundry. He did. He brought his family. From the laundry he graduated to a restaurant which became, and remains, the most popular simple eating place in town.

The waitresses, Anglos and Spanish, work under the supervision of his wife, whom they address as "mother." I remember when his son, who later served with distinction in the Army Air Force, won the soap-box derby. The reception he gave at the leading hotel in town after his daughter's marriage, and the housewarming when the family, extended by marriages and grandchildren, moved into the houses they now occupy, are considered as among the largest and most chic Santa Fe has ever known. For some years he was chairman of the local Restaurateurs' Association. In this town, there is nothing surprising in all of this, to him or to anyone else.

The Spanish settlers and conquerors, bringing with them old Spanish ways and an ancient faith, came from distant Mexico over deserts fiercer than any ocean, to conquer and convert a yet more ancient land. The Pueblo Indians had been planting their corn for centuries, and for centuries evolving their elaborate religion, the public manifestations of which, the great summer dances, are one of America's finest spectacles. For at least 2000 years men had farmed the little valleys; the art of irrigation was old and well established. Two dry-country farming peoples met. The native ones were conquered, revolted and drove out the conquerors; the Spaniards came back. In the end Indian and Spaniard settled down together to a harmonious pattern of social and cultural exchange and no little intermarriage, a pattern into which the Anglo-American newcomers are steadily merging.

These Spaniards were cut off from the world. A trip to the viceregal capital in Mexico was an adventure not to be lightly undertaken until, in recent days, the railroad and later the motor roads spanned the wastes, and the wild tribes that haunted them had been broken. North and east the mountains and prairies offered little attraction to the settler, and they, too, were thronged by wild tribes; to the west, the worst deserts of all cut the colony off from the West Coast. In speech and in customs the people kept and still keep much of 17th- and 18th-Century Spain, although in the last generation the language has decayed rapidly, soaking up English words and losing structure.

In the rural districts, old ways hold fast. The *velorio*, the lamenting wake for the dead, the wedding receptions with their great formality, vast eating and drinking, their dances led off by the bride in her wedding dress—and occasionally their fights—go on as they did 300 years ago. The people are still, by preference, wine drinkers, sweetish, heady wines, after the manner of Spain, and *cabrito*, a three-month-old kid roasted whole, remains, deservedly, a prime delicacy.

In some of the villages the *Penitentes*, a lay order with special ritual centering around Good Friday and Easter, maintain their practices. Because of excessive flagellation their rites were banned by the Catholic Church for a time, but the people refused to give them up. The present archbishop has wisely brought them under control by removing the ban and bringing the organization under the Church and into the open. Even in Santa Fe the religious processions are still maintained and the *alabados*, the traditional hymns, many of which were brought from Spain, are still sung.

West, north, and south of the Pueblo country, which was and is the main farming area, lay the various tribes of Apaches, the warriors, the raiders. They still hold to sections of their ancient range. On the Colorado border are the Jicarilla Apaches; in the southeastern part of the state, the Mescalero Apaches occupy the green, rich mountains which were once their ancient stronghold. In the northwestern corner some of the greatest of all the Apache tribes, the Navajos, are to this day trying to make a success of sheep ranching in a desert.

The Mescaleros and Jicarillas live in good grazing and timber country. They are prosperous, hard-working, and progressive. From the tourist point of view they don't offer much, as their old culture is almost gone. Some of the older Jicarilla men still wear their hair in braids, and a fair number of the women keep to the full-skirted, calico costume which became established among many tribes in the latter part of the last century. The Mescaleros offer less to the eye than that, but on the Fourth of July, if you can take hours of driving through very hot, bleak range country and rugged camping conditions, it is worth going to their celebration to see their renowned Crown Dance, a masked dance unlike any other, portraying the mountain spirits. The Jicarillas also have a masked ceremony, in which I have been allowed to participate in a very small way, but one should not try to attend uninvited.

Most people who know Apaches like them enormously and are enthusiastic about them. They are good friends and delightful companions. In the Southwest, at least, it is the common observation that Indians have a delightful sense of humor, and of all the tribes, the Apaches have the keenest and quickest. People sometimes ask me for examples, and then I am stumped, for it is not a humor of the formal joke; the things that made me laugh so hard became merely flat when repeated out of context. It is a sense of the ridiculous, kidding which is never malicious, a constant, pleased awareness that the funny side of life is also always with us and a readiness to indicate it by a quick, unexpected phrase. A form of it is in the roar of laughter that shook the medicine lodge when old Maipi, showing the young men how a certain song should be sung, lifted his voice so well that his upper plate jumped out and fell on the drum—and above all in the fact that he laughed as hard as the rest. It is in a thousand lesser, less obvious moments.

Apaches, including Navajos, are something else again when they are angry; you want to stay away from them. I remember when an Apache leader decided to put me off the reservation. Things were really sticky for a while, but fortunately there was a division of opinion, and he dropped the project. Later we became friends. When the women get angry, you want to get clear out of the country. I have seen Navajo women, in their velveteen blouses and their full, calico skirts and their jewelry, rising up one by one from where they sat behind their men in council and shouting at them to start fighting, and have watched the men's uneasy response and mounting tension. It was then that I understood why Navajo women are given such names as War Encircling, War in the Mountains, Followed to War, and Dancing for War. It was a profound relief when some influential leaders talked them down. I wasn't involved in what had made them so angry, but once they got going, I thought they might include me on principle.

By comparison with the tribes now known as Apache, the Navajos live in deep poverty on their ash heap of a desert, ever vainly presenting to the Great White Stepfather a dreadful bill of broken promises. Nonetheless, they have kept their old spirit and many of their old ways. Their big ceremonies are dances lasting all night for several nights, and most of them are held late in the fall. Attending them means driving over bad roads, rough camping, and sitting in the cold night on hard, cold ground. For those hardy enough, it is worth while. The dances, masked or unmasked, seen by the light of bonfires, the gatherings in themselves, the strange, hypnotic music—all these add up to a genuinely moving experience.

It is the Pueblos whom the tourists visit most, and with reason. Their villages are on or within easy reach of the paved highways; most conveniently, many of their dances occur annually on fixed dates. The villages, of warm, earth-colored adobe houses, are charming in themselves. The people are friendly by habit, and from long experience know how to deal with strangers. Almost all of them engage in some form of craftwork. The variety of their dances is bewildering. It is almost impossible to judge between them, but the most famous, and among the finest, are the Corn Dances of San Felipe, Cochití, and Santo Domingo, in May, July, and August. These are performed by lines of fifty or more men and women accompanied by drums and a powerful chorus.

When you attend one, you will be at first a trifle bewildered by the sheer mass, then fascinated by the costumes, the color, the music. Shortly after this you will find the performance monotonous, the sun hot, the ground hard, the dust annoying. This is the point at which many people leave. If you stay on, *and if you keep quiet,* the rhythms of drum, song, and dance, the endlessly changing formations of the lines of dancers, the very heat and dust, unite and take hold. You will realize slowly that what looked simple is complex, disciplined, sophisticated. You will forget yourself. The chances are then that you will go away with that same odd, empty, satisfied feeling which comes after absorbing any great work of art.

Simply to complete the list of the assorted elements that make up the population of the state, we should note that its northwest corner touches the southeast corner of Utah. That point is inside the Navajo Reservation, but the Mormons have filtered down into the San Juan River Valley just to the east of it. To New Mexicans, Mormons are a variety of Anglo, however they may classify themselves. Their settlements are characterized by the planting of poplars and roses; the people by industry, temperance, hospitality, and great kindness towards strangers.

The most famous and most visited part of New Mexico is the central valley, the strip along the Rio Grande from Albuquerque north past Santa Fe to Taos, guarded on the south by the Sandia, on the west by the Jémez, on the east by the Sangre de Cristo Mountains. It is an area about a hundred and fifty miles long by about sixty miles wide, possessing a special magic. Here for thousands of years people have been drawn and have stayed in the slow, sunlit peace between the mountains.

Here, as many thousands of years ago as your imagination desires, men hunted, and here they acquired the art of planting corn, squash, and beans. Other men, other tribes, joined them in one millennium or another, from the north, the east, and the west, to form the chain of settled, semicivilized villages and towns, some of them almost cities, which the Spaniards found here.

In this same area the Spaniards settled and stayed. They, too, like the Pueblos, were isolated from the ever-changing, corroding, restless currents of time. The Mountain Men, dropping down into Taos for a spree, married, built houses, became one with the country. Currents from the main stream of the Anglos' westward migration flowed in between the mountains. The valley absorbed them all.

Latterly, in the last thirty years or so, there has occurred a curious, mixed immigration of artists and anthropologists who, like so many others, came to exploit and stayed to participate. Their influence has been profound. Art and science formed a firm alliance and the two made the earlier comers aware of the riches that lay in these many times and cultures, not superimposed, but existing and interchanging side by side. It was they who stopped and reversed the existing trend to replace the native adobe architecture as rapidly as possible with commonplace brick and frame houses.

The old Mountain Men dressed in a mixture of Indian and Spanish styles because that was the kind of clothing available. The artists and their surrounding group are likely to turn up in Indian moccasins, sombreros from Old Mexico, and any combination one can imagine in between. Out of an original, Western informality they have developed an atmosphere in which everyone, of either sex, dresses as he pleases, while adaptations of Spanish and Navajo women's dresses have ceased to be merely local and have spread throughout the country.

They are a picturesque group, these latecomers, ranging from what, since Dorothy Thomas' story on the subject, is known as the "fainting robin," the starveling poet without paper or typewriter, to the—shall I call her "expatriate"?—of wealth who may become the fainting robin's patron. They include artists and scientists of national and international standing. They will join a party, go to Mexico, or take off for the Navajo country at the drop of a sombrero, are active in local politics, have fifth columns in most of the newspapers, and by and large are steady, respectable workers. The kick which they, and the Indians, get out of observing the appearance and antics of the tourists is no greater than the kick the tourists get, legitimately, out of them.

I remember, in particular, John Sloan. Since the 1920's he had been the dean of Santa Fe painters, an indestructible man, everyone thought, and a leader in every imaginable interest from renovating the annual fiesta, which had become a shabby affair, to winning the Indians their rights. The news of his death came as many of his associates, painters such as Randall Davey, Josef Bakos, and Will Shuster, were on their way to a musicale given by a woman who had been one of his good friends and patrons. The musicale went off all right, but around the drinks afterward there was a sort of silent wake, remembering the landmarks of his old, faded velveteen Navajo shirt and his silver concho belt, remembering the unconventional stunts he used to start, sometimes in that very house, and looking at his magnificent portrait of the owner. There will never be anyone else like him, but the young ones keep coming up; new movements, new art centers, new rebellions are organized annually. The art colony that stretches loosely from Albuquerque to Taos is made up of extreme individualists, but its strength is collective, and it is continuously self-renewing.

To this rich mélange the last war brought the strangest addition of all, the atomic complex. On the eastern slope of the Jémez Mountains, where the adolescents of Los Alamos Ranch School used to study their books and ride their ponies, the great center of Los Alamos was established. It has brought into the valley an increment of people, mostly young and energetic, of far higher than average intelligence, education, and artistic sensitivity.

Just outside Albuquerque are Kirtland Air Force Base and Sandia Army Base, both concerned with the new weapons. In these installations is to be found one of the highest concentrations of intellectual commissioned officers anywhere in our armed services; Army colonels and Navy commanders with Ph.D. degrees are commonplace there. Considerably farther south, in the arid, open-range cattle country, are the White Sands Proving Grounds, where they shoot off the big rockets.

It gives us a queer feeling to have these activities in New Mexico, and to have their nerve center nestled cozily in the soft grandeur of the Jémez, overlooking the heart of our timeless valley. One has a feeling of some sort of violation, yet that feeling is based upon a dream, for out of this valley, as I have said, the young men keep going to war. There has been no greater violation than that a whole regiment of New Mexico men, out of the Spanish-speaking hill villages, from the country of the drawling cowhands, from the deserts and mountains of the Indians, a whole regiment of them, should have been lost on Bataan.

All of these elements give the state its character and give it, also, its quality of being at once rawly new and richly old, the home of peaceful farmers and craftsmen when Europe was at the bottom of the Dark Ages . . . and one of the newest states, full of hope and vinegar.

It is unfortunate that an honest description cannot stop at this point. It should be enough that on a Sunday a Pueblo Indian, having spent the preceding week cultivating his red, blue, and yellow corn in his ancestral field, will put on his Indian clothes to sing in the chorus of a dance in which his daughter, who during the week works at Los Alamos, will take the part of the Buffalo Maiden, that during the performance Spanish-American neighbors will kneel in the bower at one side of the pueblo's plaza to sing *alabados* before the image of its patron saint, while artists, scientists (both anthropologists and nuclear physicists), tourists, and plain businessmen watch the performance with appreciation and respect. It should be enough, but it is not.

As in old melodramas, the lovely maiden, the happy home, are threatened by villains, of which here there are two principal ones. The first of these is a dwindling land base. In arid country, un-irrigable land is used generally for grazing, and if the grazing is not carefully controlled, the grasses are eaten up, what shoots appear are consumed before seed can form, and the grass dies away. Then the hard rains carry off the soil, until the fertility has literally been mined out of the ground. This is happening over altogether too much of New Mexico.

The second villain is race hatred. In a community such as New Mexico the opportunity to demonstrate a real melting pot is priceless, and there are sections where that demonstration is being made. There are also sections, large ones, where the reverse is true. This is particularly the case where the Texas influence is strong, but it is not confined to those areas. An Indian may or may not be Jim Crowed, according to where he happens to land, regardless of whether or not that particular town makes a big noise about its Indians for the tourist trade.

The Spanish-Americans are politically powerful and sophisticated; nonetheless they, too, encounter race hatred. In parts of the state they are truly equals, and Spanish-Anglo marriages are common; in others, notably in the south and east, they, too, encounter a frank Jim Crow system.

Neither of these villains has as yet actually obtained a mortgage on the old homestead or tied the heroine across the railroad track. They are still more threat than imminent danger; and powerful groups in the state are working to defeat them.

What is New Mexico, then? How sum it up? It is a vast, harsh, poverty-stricken, varied, and beautiful land, a breeder of artists and warriors. It is the home, by birth or by passionate adoption, of a wildly assorted population which has shown itself capable of achieving homogeneity without sacrificing its diversity. It is primitive, undeveloped, overused, new, raw, rich with tradition, old, and mellow. It is a land full of the essence of peace, although its history is one of invasions and conflicts. It is itself, an entity, at times infuriating, at times utterly delightful to its lovers, a land that draws and holds men and women with ties that cannot be explained or submitted to reason.

4

New Mexico Was Our Fate

CONRAD RICHTER

Conrad Richter (1890–1968) lived in New Mexico for over twenty years.
*Three of his novels—*The Sea of Grass, Tacey Cromwell, *and* The
Lady—*are set in the Southwest.*

It seemed inevitable that we should come to New Mexico. The first intimation, although it wasn't fully recognized then, came when I was five or six years old. A slightly older cousin and I resolved to run off West and fight the Indians. We thoughtfully accumulated food, blankets, tobacco, firearms and cartridges. These we hid in the cellar. My cousin had foolishly confided in his sister. The last night she burst into tears and gave us away. It's likely that the whipping I got wasn't so much for wanting to run away as for our cache of supplies, most of which in a spirit of joint family ownership we had set aside from the general store in which my father at that time was a partner.

The second sign, this time fairly accurate of the specific region in which we would later make our home, was while courting my future wife. Her neighbors played a certain record over and over on the phonograph. It became our theme song. The name I have forgotten but not the Spanish music. It was a Mexican song, and how it got to our Pennsylvania Dutch countryside I will never know. Blindly but surely events conspired a few years later to make us sell our Eastern farm-home, burn our bridges behind us and cast our lot on New Mexican soil.

It was perhaps the most significant move we ever made. Not for anything would we have wanted to miss the incomparably rich experience of the Southwest. From the very first we grew aware of phenomenon in sensation. We found that simple quiet scenes such as green lombardy against an *adobe* house aroused in us a vitality of feeling not to be found elsewhere. We could sit and look at it by the hour or at an old craggy cottonwood with leaves stirring lazily in the sun. We were told that this was the spirit of *mañana*, but that far from explained it. Near the end of my book, *The Mountain on The Desert*, there is speculation on the secret of this Southwestern magic known locally as enchantment.

New Mexico became our second home. We acquired a fiercer love for it than for the state in which we had been born. Coming back to it, we shouted our delight the moment our car crossed its border. The New Mexican air, we thought, tasted finer, headier. Of course, there were early difficulties. One was a constant thirst for the sight of water. I recall once stopping the car on the dirt road, now Rio Grande Boulevard, to gaze for a long time at a large pond of rainwater caught in a nearby field.

At first we also lived under a strong sense of exile, despite our finding more interesting people to the square kilometer in New Mexico than any place we had known. For example, the first house we occupied as a family had as immediate neighbors: a geologist who knew the history of the mines of the State and his wife who knew the history of the mine people; a retired rancher from the mystical Ladrón country; and a charming Spanish family, both adult members of which had been born in Mexico, the wife the daughter of a Mazatlán ship building family and a Scotch sea captain.

The Ladrón rancher, also of Spanish blood, came over to see me one day when I was in the yard.

"You have some business?" he wondered after we had talked a while.

"I write," I told him. "You know, books and magazines."

He stared at me incredulously, then shook his head.

"The things some people have to do for a living!" he commiserated.

He told me with pride about his own work on the wide Ladrón range, and his hunger for jerky since he had lived in town. He gave me my first native flavor of New Mexico. Indeed when I look back on it now, I can see what a rich bonanza of people and country that we as a writer's family had unwittingly been thrown into. When I went to the Cattle Sanitary Board to ask for the name of a man who might give me authentic material for a Western story I had in mind, they directed me to a house only a block or two down my own street. Here in a hall as wide as a room and hung with longhorns and oldtime photographs, I had the good fortune to meet a couple who had lived through many of the days of the Territory and who could tell me about them. Their names were Herbert and Lou Hardy, and very patiently they answered all my inept questions.

I did not always have such good fortune. We had come to New Mexico at a time when hundreds of men and women who had lived through the days before the railroad were still alive. I talked to many of them, and they told me what they knew. But in the case of a few, knowing something wasn't the same as being able to express it. I remember one man who had been friend and companion to a famous early character.

"Tell me about him," I said eagerly. "What was he like?"

He thought hard.

"Well, he was about five feet eight, dark complected and weighed around a hundred and sixty pounds." That was the most I could get out of him about an exciting human being.

Now the Hardys were different, articulate. That they had originally been Southerners undoubtedly helped. They could tell me what their friends and neighbors were like. Human incidents about them rose easily to their lips. When H. W. Hardy went with me to Socorro, Magdalena and other places, men crowded around to trade badinage and humor. His stories were priceless, and at this late date I want to pay tribute to his friendship and memory. It was unfortunate that Hardy's Socorro friend, whom he believed from confidences given to have been Frank Jackson of Sam Bass fame, was dead. You know the old song, *"And Jackson in the bushes a trying to get away."* But in the Hardy house I learned to know other old-timers including Bob Lewis, the fabled marshal of Magdalena.

In New Mexico two regions had the strongest influence on me. One of these was the pinal. I mean the pine belt that, as all New Mexicans know, starts below seven thousand feet elevation although much of the ponderosa at this lower altitude had long since been cut down. Our second summer in New Mexico we took a cabin in the big pines on the eastern slope of the Sandia Mountains. We found the climate at 7200 feet that first June well nigh flawless. We loved it, stayed until Christmas and came back the following spring.

Now love is a very strange and powerful thing. It seems silly to suppose that such an inanimate object as a place or region can respond to this mysterious emotion and return it. And yet, curiously enough, that is exactly what came to pass. We were in the trough of the great depression. We had lost everything and were very poor. A member of my family was not yet completely well, and a living from my pen seemed most precarious. Nevertheless the pinal took care of us. The owner of our cabin and of the nearby store, Dayton Dalbey, showed us every kindness, and the driver of the mountain laundry truck that stopped at our door urged me to come and talk to his mother who, he said, knew Billy the Kid.

Now Billy the Kid happened to be my gauge of the veracity and authenticity of early New Mexicans. If someone claimed he had known the outlaw, I found it discreet to be skeptical of many things he said. On the other hand, if he said frankly he had never seen the Kid, I listened to him with respect and confidence. So I felt reluctant to talk to this unknown mother who had known Billy the Kid. But you don't willingly rebuff the only laundryman who comes within twenty-five miles of your house. When at last I called, there sat talking quietly to me from her chair a most authentic white-haired woman whose father had kept an early stage station at Antelope Springs when the Estancia Valley was a wilderness, and whose husband later on had run a general store at Ruidoso. Here, she told me, Billy the Kid had often hidden from the law, a friend of the family who took her small boy for rides on his horse.

Her stories about Billy the Kid, while interesting, still left me cold, although not so cold as he had left many who had incurred his displeasure. On the other hand, what she told me of her life as a girl during the sixties in her father's dot of habitation on this wild and lonely land moved me deeply. Her father couldn't leave the station, and she and her brother, neither of them more than children, used to drive the wagon to Santa Fe for supplies. It was then a trip of several days. They would camp far from the trail at night, not daring to light a fire for fear of the Apaches.

She gave me such a picture of herself and her brother that they made their way into my next story. Under the name of *Early Marriage* it took me into the *Post,* the first of a New Mexican series. The name of the laundryman who knocked on my door with such good fortune was Alfred Dow. It seems peculiarly American that a boy whose family had sheltered Billy the Kid from officers of the law should later become an officer himself and a member of the New Mexico State Police. (Alfred M. Dow is a veteran member of the New Mexico State Police. His pioneer mother, Isabel McAttee Dow was born Jan. 4, 1861, died Oct. 8, 1948, at the age of 87.)

If this were all that the New Mexican pinal had done for me, I would have reason enough to be grateful. But W. T. Boyd, a neighbor at Sandia Park, brought over two books for me to read. They were old and somewhat tattered, revealing none of the ultimate richness of the gesture. The books were Henry Howe's monumental historical collection of early Ohio first published in 1840. I read them by gasoline lantern light to the sound of wind in the pines. A new world of life in the deep forests of the early Midwest was opened to me. Out of it came my Ohio trilogy, first conceived and planned at 7200 feet in the big timber of the Sandias which, I think, helped me to understand the big timber of a life 150 years and 1500 miles away.

The other region of New Mexico that returned my love was the grasslands. They had made a strong impression on me from the moment I had looked out of the Santa Fe car window and seen the great green meadows around Las Vegas and, a few hours later, the Glorieta country like a vast park planned on a monumental scale and planted with ornamental evergreens. Later on at Albuquerque we used to drive the many wheel tracks that threaded the then lonely and uninhabited outer *mesa.* Another favorite spot was a trail from Corrales up over the sand hills where the grass of those luxuriant summers of the early thirties ran on and on with no sign of life but grazing cattle and horses.

More and more the beauty, mystery and immensity of the grasslands got into my blood. The Hardys and others had told me about the San Augustine Plains, and I had explored them myself. But it was while driving to Quay County one day to see a man named Griggs, who told me many wonderful things from his long experience with western horses, that the impulse to put it into a long story came to me. It had been a rainy summer. Beyond Vaughn I found a green paradise of grassland, rolling, pitching, dipping, rising, fresh and fertile, studded with small ponds and flowing with milk and honey. That was where *The Sea of Grass* first took hold of my mind.

New Mexico has given me so much and there is so little space to tell it, but this testament of love can't be closed without mention of my gratitude to some others of its people. Agnes Morley Cleaveland, Judge C. M. Botts, Will Keleher, Ruth Laughlin Alexander, Thomas Matthew Pierce, Erna Fergusson, S. Omar Barker, to name only a few of the many who encouraged me and who have left the warm glow of New Mexico on the heart.

5

New Mexico

D. H. LAWRENCE

D. H. Lawrence spent the fall and winter of 1922–23 and the spring and summer of 1925 in Taos, New Mexico.

Superficially, the world has become small and known. Poor little globe of earth, the tourists trot round you as easily as they trot round the Bois or round Central Park. There is no mystery left, we've been there, we've seen it, we know all about it. We've done the globe, and the globe is done.

This is quite true, superficially. On the superficies, horizontally, we've been everywhere and done everything, we know all about it. Yet the more we know, superficially, the less we penetrate, vertically. It's all very well skimming across the surface of the ocean, and saying you know all about the sea. There still remain the terrifying underdeeps, of which we have utterly no experience.

The same is true of land travel. We skim along, we get there, we see it all, we've done it all. And as a rule, we never once go through the curious film which railroads, ships, motorcars, and hotels over the surface of the whole earth. Peking is just the same as New York, with a few different things to look at; rather more Chinese about, etc. Poor creatures that we are, we crave for experience, yet we are like flies that crawl on the pure and transparent mucous-paper in which the world like a bon-bon is wrapped so carefully that we can never get at it, though we see it there all the time as we move about it, apparently in contact, yet actually as far removed as if it were the moon.

As a matter of fact, our great-grandfathers, who never went anywhere, in actuality had more experience of the world than we have, who have seen everything. When they listened to a lecture with lantern-slides, they really held their breath before the unknown, as they sat in the village school-room. We, bowling along in a rickshaw in Ceylon, say to ourselves: "It's very much what you'd expect." We really know it all.

We are mistaken. The know-it-all state of mind is just the result of being outside the mucous-paper wrapping of civilization. Underneath is everything we don't know and are afraid of knowing.

I realized this with shattering force when I went to New Mexico.

New Mexico, one of the United States, part of the U.S.A. New Mexico, the picturesque reservation and playground of the eastern states, very romantic, old Spanish, Red Indian, desert mesas, pueblos, cowboys, penitentes, all that film-stuff. Very nice, the great South-West, put on a sombrero and knot a red kerchief round your neck, to go out in the great free spaces!

That is New Mexico wrapped in the absolutely hygienic and shiny mucous-paper of our trite civilization. That is the New Mexico known to most of the Americans who know it at all. But break through the shiny sterilized wrapping, and actually *touch* the country, and you will never be the same again.

I think New Mexico was the greatest experience from the outside world that I have ever had. It certainly changed me for ever. Curious as it may sound, it was New Mexico that liberated me from the present era of civilization, the great era of material and mechanical development. Months spent in holy Kandy, in Ceylon, the holy of holies of Southern Buddhism, had not touched the great psyche of materialism and idealism which dominated me. And years, even in the exquisite beauty of Sicily, right among the old Greek paganism that still lives there, had not shattered the essential Christianity on which my character was established. Australia was a sort of dream or trance, like being under a spell, the self remaining unchanged, so long as the trance did not last too long. Tahiti, in a mere glimpse, repelled me; and so did California, after a stay of a few weeks. There seemed a strange brutality in the spirit of the western coast, and I felt: O, let me get away!

But the moment I saw the brilliant, proud morning shine high up over the deserts of Santa Fe, something stood still in my soul, and I started to attend. There was a certain magnificence in the high-up day, a certain eagle-like royalty, so different from the equally pure, equally pristine and lovely morning of Australia, which is so soft, so utterly pure in its softness, and betrayed by green parrot flying. But in the lovely morning of Australia one went into a dream. In the magnificent fierce morning of New Mexico one sprang awake, a new part of the soul woke up suddenly, and the old world gave way to a new.

There are all kinds of beauty in the world, thank God, though ugliness is homogeneous. How lovely is Sicily, with Calabria across the sea like an opal, and Etna with her snow in a world above and beyond! How lovely is Tuscany, with little red tulips wild among the corn: or bluebells at dusk in England, or mimosa in clouds of pure yellow among the grey-green dun foliage of Australia, under a soft, blue, unbreathed sky! But for a *greatness* of beauty I have never experienced anything like New Mexico. All those mornings when I went with a hoe along the ditch to the Cañon, at the ranch, and stood, in the fierce, proud silence of the Rockies, on their foothills, to look far over the desert to the blue mountains away in Arizona, blue as chalcedony, with the sage-brush desert sweeping grey-blue in between, dotted with tiny cube-crystals of houses, the vast amphitheatre of lofty, indomitable desert, sweeping round to the ponderous Sangre de Cristo mountains on the east, and coming up flush at the pine-dotted foot-hills of the Rockies! What splendor! Only the tawny eagle could really sail out into the splendor of it all. Leo Stein once wrote to me: It is the most aesthetically-satisfying landscape I know. To me it was much more than that. It had a splendid silent terror, and a vast far-and-wide magnificence which made it way beyond mere aesthetic appreciation. Never is the light more pure and overweening than there, arching with a royalty almost cruel over the hollow, uptilted world. For it is curious that the land which had produced modern political democracy as its highest pitch should give one of the greatest sense of overweening, terrible proudness and mercilessness: but so beautiful, God! so beautiful! Those that have spent morning after morning alone there pitched among the pines above the great proud world of desert will know, almost unbearably how beautiful it is, how clear and unquestioned is the might of the day. Just day itself is tremendous there. It is so easy to understand that the Aztecs gave hearts of men to the sun. For the sun is not merely hot or scorching, not at all. It is of a brilliant and unchallengeable purity and haughty serenity which would make one sacrifice the heart to it. Ah, yes, in New Mexico the heart is sacrificed to the sun and the human being is left stark, heartless, but undauntedly religious.

And that was the second revelation out there. I had looked over all the world for something that would strike *me* as religious. The simple piety of some English people, the semi-pagan mystery of some Catholics in southern Italy, the intensity of some Bavarian peasants, the semi-ecstasy of Buddhists or Brahmins: all this had seemed religious all right, as far as the parties concerned were involved, but it didn't involve me. I looked on at the religiousness from the outside. For it is still harder to feel religion at will than to love at will.

I had seen what I felt was a hint of wild religion in the so-called devil dances of a group of naked villagers from the far-remote jungle in Ceylon, dancing at midnight under the torches, glittering wet with sweat on their dark bodies as if they had been gilded, at the celebration of the Pera-hera, in Kandy, given to the Prince of Wales. And the utter dark absorption of these naked men, as they danced with their knees wide apart suddenly affected me with a *sense* of religion. I *felt* religion for a moment. For religion is an experience, an uncontrollable sensual experience, even more so than love: I use sensual to mean an experience deep down in the senses, inexplicable and inscrutable.

But this experience was fleeting, gone in the curious turmoil of the Pera-hera, and I had no permanent feeling of religion till I came to New Mexico and penetrated into the old human race-experience there. It is curious that it should be in America, of all places, that a European should really experience religion, after touching the old Mediterranean and the East. It is curious that one should get a sense of living religion from the Red Indians, having failed to get it from Hindus or Sicilian Catholics or Cingalese.

Let me make a reservation. I don't stand up to praise the Red Indian as he reveals himself in contact with white civilization. From that angle, I am forced to admit he *may* be thoroughly objectionable. Even my small experience knows it. But also I know he *may* be thoroughly nice, even in his dealings with white men. It's a question of individuals, a good deal, on both sides.

But in this article, I don't want to deal with the everyday or superficial aspect of New Mexico, outside the mucous-paper wrapping, I *want* to go beneath the surface. But therefore the American Indian in his behavior as an American citizen doesn't really concern me. What concerns me is what he is—or what he seems to me to be, in his ancient, ancient race-self and religious-self.

For the Red Indian seems to me much older than Greeks, or Hindus or any European or even Egyptians. The Red Indian, as a civilized and truly religious man, civilized beyond taboo and totem, as he is in the south, is religious in perhaps the oldest sense, and deepest, of the word. That is to say, he is a remnant of the most religious race still living. So it seems to me.

But again let me protect myself. The Indian who sells you baskets on Albuquerque station or who slinks around Taos plaza may be an utter waster and an indescribably low dog. Personally he may be even less religious than a New York sneak-thief. He may have broken with his tribe, or his tribe itself may have collapsed finally from its old religious integrity, and ceased, really to exist. Then he is only fit for rapid absorption into white civilization, which must make the best of him.

But while a tribe retains its religion and keeps up its religious practices, and while any member of the tribe shares in those practices, then there is a tribal integrity and a living tradition going back far beyond the birth of Christ, beyond the pyramids, beyond Moses. A vast old religion which once swayed the earth lingers in unbroken practice there in New Mexico, older, perhaps, than anything in the world save Australian aboriginal taboo and totem, and that is not yet religion.

You can feel it, the atmosphere of it, around the pueblos. Not, of course, when the place is crowded with sight-seers and motor-cars. But go to Taos pueblo on some brilliant snowy morning and see the white figure on the roof: or come riding through at dusk on some windy evening, when the black skirts of the silent women blow around the white wide boots, and you will feel the old, old root of human consciousness still reaching down to depths we know nothing of: and of which, only too often, we are jealous. It seems it will not be long before the pueblos are uprooted.

But never shall I forget watching the dancers, the men with the fox-skin swaying down from their buttocks, file out at San Geronimo, and the women with seed rattles following. The long, streaming, glistening black hair of the men. Even in ancient Crete long hair was sacred in a man, as it is still in the Indians. Never shall I forget the utter absorption of the dance, so quiet, so steadily, timelessly rhythmic, and silent, with the ceaseless down-tread, always to the earth's centre, the very reverse of the upflow of Dionysiac or Christian ecstasy. Never shall I forget the deep singing of the men at the drum, swelling and sinking, the deepest sound I have heard in all my life, deeper than thunder, deeper than the sound of the Pacific Ocean, deeper than the roar of a deep waterfall: the wonderful deep sound of men calling to the unspeakable depths.

Never shall I forget coming into the little pueblo of San Filipi one sunny morning in spring, unexpectedly, when bloom was on the trees in the perfect little pueblo more old, more utterly peaceful and idyllic than anything in Theocritus, and seeing a little casual dance. Not impressive as a spectacle, only, to me, profoundly moving because of the truly terrifying religious absorption of it.

Never shall I forget the Christmas dances at Taos, twilight, snow, the darkness coming over the great wintry mountains and the lonely pueblo, then suddenly, again, like dark calling to dark, the deep Indian cluster-singing around the drum, wild and awful, suddenly arousing on the last dusk as the procession starts. And then the bon-fires leaping suddenly in pure spurts of high flame, columns of sudden flame forming an alley for the procession.

Never shall I forget the khiva of birch-trees, away in the Apache country, in Arizona this time, the tepees and flickering fires, the neighing of horses unseen under the huge dark night, and the Apaches all abroad in their silent moccasined feet: and in the khiva beyond a little fire, the old man reciting, reciting in an unknown Apache speech, in the strange wild Indian voice that re-echoes away back to before the Flood, reciting apparently the traditions and legends of the tribe, going on and on, while the young men, the *braves* of today, wandered in, listened, and wandered away again, overcome with the power and majesty of that utterly old tribal voice, yet uneasy with their half-adherence to the modern civilization, the two things in contact. And one of the *braves* shoved his face under my hat, in the night, and stared with his glittering eyes close to mine. He'd have killed me then and there, had he dared. He didn't dare: and I knew it: and he knew it.

Never shall I forget the Indian races, when the young men, even the boys, run naked, smeared with white earth and stuck with bits of eagle fluff for the swiftness of the heavens, and the old men brush them with eagle feathers, to give them power. And they run in the strange hurling fashion of the primitive world, hurled forward, not making speed deliberately. And the race is not for victory. It is not a contest. There is no competition. It is a great cumulative effort. The tribe this day is adding up its male energy and exerting it to the utmost—for what? To get power, to get strength: to come, by sheer cumulative, hurling effort of the bodies of men, into contact with the great cosmic source of vitality which gives strength, power, energy to the men who can grasp it, energy for the zeal of attainment.

It was a vast old religion, greater than anything we know: more starkly and nakedly religious. There is no God, no conception of a god. All is god. But it is not the pantheism we are accustomed to, which expresses itself as "God is everywhere, God is in everything." In the oldest religion, everything was alive, not supernaturally but naturally alive. There were only deeper and deeper streams of life, vibrations of life more and more vast. So rocks were alive, but a mountain had a deeper, vaster life than a rock, and it was much harder for a man to bring his spirit, or his energy, into contact with the life of the mountain, and so draw strength from the mountain, as from a great standing well of life, than it was to come into contact with the rock. And he had to put forth a great religious effort. For the whole life-effort of man was to get his life into direct contact with the elemental life of the cosmos, mountain-life, cloud-life, thunder-life, air-life, earth-life, sun-life. To come into immediate *felt* contact, and so derive energy, power, and a dark sort of joy. This effort into sheer naked contact, *without an intermediary or mediator*, is the root meaning of religion, and at the sacred races the runners hurled themselves in a terrible cumulative effort, through the air, to come at last into naked contact with the very life of air, which is the life of the clouds, and so of the rain.

It was a vast and pure religion, without idols or images, even mental ones. It is the oldest religion, a cosmic religion the same for all peoples, not broken up into specific gods or saviours or systems. It is the religion which precedes the god-concept, and is therefore greater and deeper than any god-religion.

And it lingers still, for a little while in New Mexico: but long enough to have been a revelation to me. And the Indian, however objectionable he may be on occasion, has still some of the strange beauty and pathos of the religion that brought him forth and is now shedding him away into oblivion. When Trinidad, the Indian boy, and I planted corn at the ranch, my soul paused to see his brown hands softly moving the earth over the maize in pure ritual. He was back in his old religious self, and the ages stood still. Ten minutes later he was making a fool of himself with the horses. Horses were never part of the Indian's religious life, never would be. He hasn't a tithe of feeling for them that he has for a bear, for example. So horses don't like Indians.

But there it is: the newest democracy ousting the oldest religion! And once the oldest religion is ousted, one feels the democracy and all its paraphernalia will collapse, and the oldest religion, which comes down to us from man's pre-war days, will start again. The skyscraper will scatter on the winds like thistledown, and the genuine America, the America of New Mexico, will start on its course again. This is an interregnum.

6

The Pueblo Indians

C. G. JUNG

C. G. Jung (1875–1961), the influential Swiss psychologist and
psychiatrist, visited New Mexico in 1924–25.

We always require an outside point to stand on, in order to
apply the lever of criticism. This is especially so in psychology,
where by the nature of the material we are much more subjec-
tively involved than in any other science. How, for example, can we
become conscious of national peculiarities if we have never had
the opportunity to regard our own nation from outside? Regarding it from outside means regarding it from the standpoint of
another nation. To do so, we must acquire sufficient knowledge of
the foreign collective psyche, and in the course of this process of
assimilation we encounter all those incompatibilities which
constitute the national bias and the national peculiarity. Everything that irritates us about others can lead us to an understanding of ourselves. I understand England only when I see where I, as
a Swiss, do not fit in. I understand Europe, our greatest problem,
only when I see where I as a European do not fit into the world.
Through my acquaintance with many Americans, and my trips to
and in America, I have obtained an enormous amount of insight
into the European character; it has always seemed to me that
there can be nothing more useful for a European than some time

From *Memories, Dreams, Reflections,* by C. G. Jung, recorded and edited by Aniela Jaffe and
translated by Richard and Clara Winston. Copyright © 1963 by Random House, Inc.
Reprinted by permission of Pantheon Books, a Division of Random House, Inc.

or another to look out at Europe from the top of a skyscraper. When I contemplated for the first time the European spectacle from the Sahara, surrounded by a civilization which has more or less the same relationship to ours as Roman antiquity has to modern times, I became aware of how completely, even in America, I was still caught up and imprisoned in the cultural consciousness of the white man. The desire then grew in me to carry the historical comparisons still farther by descending to a still lower cultural level.

On my next trip to the United States I went with a group of American friends to visit the Indians of New Mexico, the city-building Pueblos. "City," however, is too strong a word. What they build are in reality only villages; but their crowded houses piled one atop the other suggest the word "city," as do their language and their whole manner. There for the first time I had the good fortune to talk with a non-European, that is, to a non-white. He was a chief of the Taos pueblos, an intelligent man between the ages of forty and fifty. His name was Ochwiay Biano (Mountain Lake). I was able to talk with him as I have rarely been able to talk with a European. To be sure, he was caught up in his world just as much as a European is in his, but what a world it was! In talk with a European, one is constantly running up on the sand bars of things long known but never understood; with this Indian, the vessel floated freely on deep, alien seas. At the same time, one never knows which is more enjoyable: catching sight of new shores, or discovering new approaches to age-old knowledge that has been almost forgotten.

"See," Ochwiay Biano said, "how cruel the whites look. Their lips are thin, their noses sharp, their faces furrowed and distorted by folds. Their eyes have a staring expression; they are always seeking something. What are they seeking? The whites always want something; they are always uneasy and restless. We do not know what they want. We do not understand them. We think that they are mad."

I asked him why he thought the whites were all mad.

"They say that they think with their heads," he replied.

"Why of course. What do you think with?" I asked him in surprise.

"We think here," he said, indicating his heart.

I fell into a long meditation. For the first time in my life, so it seemed to me, someone had drawn for me a picture of the real white man. It was as though until now I had seen nothing but sentimental, prettified color prints. This Indian had struck our vulnerable spot, unveiled a truth to which we are blind. I felt rising within me like a shapeless mist something unknown and yet deeply familiar. And out of this mist, image upon image detached itself: first Roman legions smashing into the cities of Gaul, and the keenly incised features of Julius Caesar, Scipio Africanus, and Pompey. I saw the Roman eagle on the North Sea and on the banks of the White Nile. Then I saw St. Augustine transmitting the Christian creed to the Britons on the tips of Roman lances, and Charlemagne's most glorious forced conversions of the heathen; then the pillaging and murdering bands of the Crusading armies. With a secret stab I realized the hollowness of that old romanticism about the Crusades. Then followed Columbus, Cortes, and the other conquistadors who with fire, sword, torture, and Christianity came down upon even these remote pueblos dreaming peacefully in the Sun, their Father. I saw, too, the peoples of the Pacific islands decimated by firewater, syphilis, and scarlet fever carried in the clothes the missionaries forced on them.

It was enough. What we from our point of view call colonization, missions to the heathen, spread of civilization, etc., has another face—the face of a bird of prey seeking with cruel intentness for distant quarry—a face worthy of a race of pirates and highwaymen. All the eagles and other predatory creatures that adorn our coats of arms seem to me apt psychological representatives of our true nature.

Something else that Ochwiay Biano said to me stuck in my mind. It seems to me so intimately connected with the peculiar atmosphere of our interview that my account would be incomplete if I failed to mention it. Our conversation took place on the roof of the fifth story of the main building. At frequent intervals figures of other Indians could be seen on the roofs, wrapped in their woolen blankets, sunk in contemplation of the wandering sun that daily rose into a clear sky. Around us were grouped the low-built square buildings of air-dried brick (adobe), with the characteristic ladders that reach from the ground to the roof, or from roof to roof of the higher stories. (In earlier, dangerous times the entrance used to be through the roof.) Before us the rolling plateau of Taos (about seven thousand feet above sea level) stretched to the horizon, where several conical peaks (ancient volcanoes) rose to over twelve thousand feet. Behind us a clear stream purled past the houses, and on its opposite bank stood a second pueblo of reddish adobe houses, built one atop the other toward the center of the settlement, thus strangely anticipating the perspective of an American metropolis with its skyscrapers in the center. Perhaps half an hour's journey upriver rose a mighty isolated mountain, *the* mountain, which has no name. The story goes that on days when the mountain is wrapped in clouds the men vanish in that direction to perform mysterious rites.

The Pueblo Indians are unusually closemouthed, and in matters of their religion absolutely inaccessible. They make it a policy to keep their religious practices a secret, and this secret is so strictly guarded that I abandoned as hopeless any attempt at direct questioning. Never before had I run into such an atmosphere of secrecy; the religions of civilized nations today are all accessible; their sacraments have long ago ceased to be mysteries. Here, however, the air was filled with a secret known to all the communicants, but to which whites could gain no access. This strange situation gave me an inkling of Eleusis, whose secret was known to one nation and yet never betrayed. I understood what Pausanias or Herodotus felt when he wrote: "I am not permitted to name the name of that god." This was not, I felt, mystification, but a vital mystery whose betrayal might bring about the downfall of the community as well as of the individual. Preservation of the secret gives the Pueblo Indian pride and the power to resist the dominant whites. It gives him cohesion and unity; and I feel sure that the Pueblos as an individual community will continue to exist as long as their mysteries are not desecrated.

It was astonishing to me to see how the Indian's emotions change when he speaks of his religious ideas. In ordinary life he shows a degree of self-control and dignity that borders on fatalistic equanimity. But when he speaks of things that pertain to his mysteries, he is in the grip of a surprising emotion which he cannot conceal—a fact which greatly helped to satisfy my curiosity. As I have said, direct questioning led to nothing. When, therefore, I wanted to know about essential matters, I made tentative remarks and observed my interlocutor's expression for those affective movements which are so very familiar to me. If I had hit on something essential, he remained silent or gave an evasive reply, but with all the signs of profound emotion; frequently tears would fill his eyes. Their religious conceptions are not theories to them (which, indeed, would have to be very curious theories to evoke tears from a man), but facts, as important and moving as the corresponding external realities.

As I sat with Ochwiay Biano on the roof, the blazing sun rising higher and higher, he said, pointing to the sun, "Is not he who moves there our father? How can anyone say differently? How can there be another god? Nothing can be without the sun." His excitement, which was already perceptible, mounted still higher; he struggled for words, and exclaimed at last, "What would a man do alone in the mountains? He cannot even build his fire without him."

I asked him whether he did not think the sun might be a fiery ball shaped by an invisible god. My question did not even arouse astonishment, let alone anger. Obviously it touched nothing within him; he did not even think my question stupid. It merely left him cold. I had the feeling that I had come upon an insurmountable wall. His only reply was, "The sun is God. Everyone can see that."

Although no one can help feeling the tremendous impress of the sun, it was a novel and deeply affecting experience for me to see these mature, dignified men in the grip of an overmastering emotion when they spoke of it.

Another time I stood by the river and looked up at the mountains, which rise almost another six thousand feet above the plateau. I was just thinking that this was the roof of the American continent, and that people lived here in the face of the sun like the Indians who stood wrapped in blankets on the highest roofs of the pueblo, mute and absorbed in the sight of the sun. Suddenly a deep voice, vibrant with suppressed emotion, spoke from behind me into my left ear: "Do you not think that all life comes from the mountain?" An elderly Indian had come up to me, inaudible in his moccasins, and had asked me this heaven knows how far-reaching question. A glance at the river pouring down from the mountain showed me the outward image that had engendered this conclusion. Obviously all life came from the mountain, for where there is water, there is life. Nothing could be more obvious. In his question, I felt a swelling emotion connected with the word "mountain," and thought of the tale of secret rites celebrated on the mountain. I replied, "Everyone can see that you speak the truth."

Unfortunately, the conversation was soon interrupted, and so I did not succeed in attaining any deeper insight into the symbolism of water and mountain.

I observed that the Pueblo Indians, reluctant as they were to speak about anything concerning their religion, talked with great readiness and intensity about their relations with the Americans. "Why," Mountain Lake said, "do the Americans not let us alone? Why do they want to forbid our dances? Why do they make difficulties when we want to take our young people from school in order to lead them to the *kiva* (site of the rituals), and instruct them in our religion? We do nothing to harm the Americans!" After a prolonged silence he continued, "The Americans want to stamp out our religion. Why can they not let us alone? What we do, we do not only for ourselves but for the Americans also. Yes, we do it for the whole world. Everyone benefits by it."

I could observe from his excitement that he was alluding to some extremely important element of his religion. I therefore asked him: "You think, then, that what you do in your religion benefits the whole world?" He replied with great animation, "Of course. If we did not do it, what would become of the world?" And with a significant gesture he pointed to the sun.

I felt that we were approaching extremely delicate ground here, verging on the mysteries of the tribe. "After all," he said, "we are a people who live on the roof of the world; we are the sons of Father Sun, and with our religion we daily help our father to go across the sky. We do this not only for ourselves, but for the whole world. If we were to cease practicing our religion, in ten years the sun would no longer rise.Then it would be night forever."

I then realized on what the "dignity," the tranquil composure of the individual Indian, was founded. It springs from his being a son of the sun; his life is cosmologically meaningful, for he helps the father and preserver of all life in his daily rise and descent. If we set against this our own self-justifications, the meaning of our own lives as it is formulated by our reason, we cannot help but see our poverty. Out of sheer envy we are obliged to smile at the Indians' naïveté and to plume ourselves on our cleverness; for otherwise we would discover how impoverished and down at the heels we are. Knowledge does not enrich us; it removes us more and more from the mythic world in which we were once at home by right of birth.

If for a moment we put away all European rationalism and transport ourselves into the clear mountain air of that solitary plateau, which drops off on one side into the broad continental prairies and on the other into the Pacific Ocean; if we also set aside our intimate knowledge of the world and exchange it for a horizon that seems immeasurable, and an ignorance of what lies beyond it, we will begin to achieve an inner comprehension of the Pueblo Indian's point of view. "All life comes from the mountain" is immediately convincing to him, and he is equally certain that he lives upon the roof of an immeasurable world, closest to God. He above all others has the Divinity's ear, and his ritual act will reach the distant sun soonest of all. The holiness of mountains, the revelation of Yahweh upon Sinai, the inspiration that Nietzsche was vouchsafed in the Engadine—all speak the same language. The idea, absurd to us, that a ritual act can magically affect the sun is, upon closer examination, no less irrational but far more familiar to us than might at first be assumed. Our Christian religion—like every other, incidentally—is permeated by the idea that special acts or a special kind of action can influence God—for example, through certain rites or by prayer, or by a morality pleasing to the Divinity.

The ritual acts of man are an answer and reaction to the action of God upon man; and perhaps they are not only that, but are also intended to be "activating," a form of magic coercion. That man feels capable of formulating valid replies to the overpowering influence of God, and that he can render back something which is essential even to God, induces pride, for it raises the human individual to the dignity of a metaphysical factor. "God and us"—even if it is only an unconscious *sous-entendu*—this equation no doubt underlies that enviable serenity of the Pueblo Indian. Such a man is in the fullest sense of the word in his proper place.

7

A Calendar of Santa Fe

WINFIELD TOWNLEY SCOTT

Winfield Townley Scott (1910–68), a major American poet, spent his last years in Santa Fe, coming from Providence, Rhode Island, where he had been literary editor of the Journal, *1941–51.*

The health of the eye seems to demand a horizon. We
are never tired, so long as we can see far enough.
—Emerson

September

If, as I intend, I go on living in New Mexico, I suppose I shall
know it far better than I do now, but I suppose I shall never again
see it as clearly as during my first year. And what is there about
this land which sets travelers to altering their schedules and
overstaying? What is there, more forcefully still, that has seized
upon astonishing numbers of people who came to look, and then
put down their luggage and remained? As it has upon me. I had
no intention of living here. When in late August we drove
through a hurricane out of our Connecticut village—my wife,
three of my children, with eleven pieces of flimsy baggage, and
trustful that though New London was flooded we might get a train
in Hartford—we were leaving for a year. I had lived all my more
than forty years in New England, I wanted a change, and I wanted
to see the Southwest.

Chambers of Commerce, or one state office or another, every now and then receive requests from citizens elsewhere in the United States for information as to the passport regulations for entering New Mexico. Spiritually, so to speak, the ignoramuses are perhaps not altogether in error. If you were flown here blindfolded—not to the cities of New Mexico, but to any of the little mountain villages with their low adobe houses, their farmers with creased Spanish faces, their herds of sheep and wandering horses—you would justifiably assume you were in a foreign land. And even in the cities, particularly in Santa Fe, there are neighborhoods that could be quite as deceptive.

This old-world look, in such plenitude, of course provides a large part of the charm of the place; and the look is native, true, not a deliberation of quaintness. Yet I think, first of all, the magic is in the land itself, the magnificent stretches and towers of land. Travelers merely passing through New Mexico on the quickest ground routes see from the cars of the Santa Fe Railroad or driving along Route 66 little but the tiring wastelands of the state; save, far west toward Gallup, a run of astounding bastions of red clay which look as though they had founded Norman and Gothic architecture. To see this aridity thrust up into awesome dramatics of landscape, you must go north to Santa Fe between the great ranges of the Jémez Mountains to the west and the Sangre de Cristos to the east, then farther north to Taos on the road which winds above the Rio Grande and beneath black buttresses of volcanic rock; or northwest over the Rio Grande, you must climb and wind through dinosauric country of mesas and canyons toward Los Alamos, which glitters like a new kind of metallic snake along the ancient earth.

The breadth and height of the land, its huge self and its huge sky, strike you like a blow. There are those who at once dislike it; in a kind of dismay at so much inhuman space, they flee from it. There are more who at first can do nothing but stand and stare. Yes, I thought, this is a part of my country and wholly different from the countryside I have so long known; this is what I expected without really being able to imagine it. Wind-blown, dry, half-barren, shining, the landscape vaulted about us as our friends drove us to Santa Fe from the station at Lamy.

The main street of our white-clapboarded, white-steepled

Connecticut village runs along a hilltop seven hundred feet above sea level: "High as Peterborough, New Hampshire," we'd boast. But here we were flung seven thousand feet above sea level. For the first week or two you can be, as I was, literally dizzied and breathless. And for three to five thousand feet more the Sangre de Cristo Mountains rise close against the eastern sky. The mountains go up. Gertrude Stein said the thing about skyscrapers is how they come down out of the sky. Mountains go up. You never see a mountain right beside you. It is always too near or too far.

By mid-September the mountaintops began to go gold with the aspen trees. Aspens grow, but rarely, at the Santa Fe height—they need another couple of thousand feet. Elm, lilac, locust, spruce, poplar: there was much right around us of familiar trees; and woodbine for remembrance; but I had to learn about the silver-gray Russian olive trees floating above adobe walls, about the pink-broom tamarisk and the lolling cottonwood, and on all the hillsides the piñon, its gnarled low growth, and the bare spaces, as it is with stars, between the piñon. The miniature forests, as Haniel Long called them, look as though they were planted. They bear tiny nuts with stone-hard shells, and they are the principal firewood, which, as it burns, so spicily scents the air.

There was gold, too, all around us in the wild bush called chamisa which smells rotten; but as to looks, it is a coronet on the dusty, hard-packed, nearly grassless, terra-cotta ground.

Several late-afternoon showers came quick and hard, but only after three weeks did we at last have a familiar-feeling, Connecticut kind of day, an overcast day. It began with small streaks above both mountain ranges and, while sunlight stayed bright, built up a cover of gray all morning on the hundreds of miles of sky. Even at noon there were great patches of blue in the west and northwest. The wind kept rising, rattling the leaves of an experimental aspen by our house and seething in the tamarisks just beyond. By midafternoon the clouds closed and blackened. There was a violent thunderstorm which soon quieted into several hours' rain. The rain shuts in the land, reduces it out of recognition—or, for us, into recognition of size we are used to. Next morning, the dust all laid, we could see the peaks of the Jémez Mountains over a long range of cloud, gray and white-edged in the early sun.

The sudden start and strength of winds here make one feel the facts of astronomy. In cozier country it seems that the sun rises and sets, the moon rises and sets, above a still and level world. But here, as on a great ship, you are more aware of the voyaging planet—the mountains wheeling upward to the sun, and the winds like encountered currents breaking across the turning earth.

October

As a New Englander, I have had to reorder my whole sense of scale. I remember that the first night we were in Santa Fe—we had been driven, late afternoon, directly to our rented house on the Camino del Monte Sol and had not been into the center of the city—I stepped out onto the road and looked at a cluster of lights in the northwest. I assumed they were the lights of downtown Santa Fe. It was several days before I discovered they were the lights of Los Alamos, thirty-five miles away, and that the Jémez Mountains I looked at with a casual admiration out our west window were fifty miles away. This would be, back East, like standing in Providence and looking at Boston.

On the other hand, what they call rivers here would hardly pass as respectable brooks back home—that is, if they were running at all.

In this staggering spaciousness of earth and sky, light is the vital force, the nervous or majestic rhythm, the master painter. In October the late-afternoon light performs dramatic things. It will turn the Jémez Range into a two-dimensional colossal backdrop, pigeon-indigo. It fires all the ridges of the foothills while shadows fill up the infolding erosions. And at that time of day, if you drive within the Sangre de Cristo Mountains, you repeatedly drive into deep shadows and yet always with ways east or south to see out, as it were, to other peaks blazing in sunlight. The golden aspens quiver along the amazing blue intersections of the sky.

The land repeats its gold everywhere. Walking the Arroyo Hondo, which has a brook and green, grassy places, I saw dandelions, a yellow cinquefoil I cannot name, the sculptured mullein, chamisa, cactus with its yellow budlike growths, and even yellow butterflies and olive-yellow birds; and from the depths of the canyon I could still see the aspens, high in the distance. When sunset comes quickly on, rose and lavender light flushes the whole eastern range as it did when the conquistadors, marveling at it, named the mountains Blood of Christ.

Across the thin air and big sky, moonlight here is titanic. Before you see the moon, but as it is rising behind the Sangre de Cristos, a glowing milkiness fills the hollows behind the near, dark foothills. When at last the moon is loosed over the peaks, the clay land emphasizes its hushing brilliance. Friends of ours from New York rode their horses out to the desert lands beyond Tesuque, just north of us, to see that vast waste in full moonlight; but they say it was like an evaporation, it was like gazing into nothingness. There was no frame of reference. Nothing but a mist of pearl. On the Camino, I like to stand in it for a while for its imposed silence, broken now and then by a dog barking in the foothills, then the bells of Cristo Rey Church running a few bars of "Ave Maria" before striking the hour.

I have said "the ancient land." It strikes a New Englander as ancient, for it shows its rocky bones, it is tall, it is undomesticated. I feel here as never before the indifference of the earth. And these mountains, softened, except at their highest Truchas Peaks, with aspen and pine, are indeed the oldest part of the Rockies. But in fact this land is much younger than New England: it had the sea long after we had it in our valleys and among—or over—our hills; it is a land all scattered with fossils for the finding, with their crustacean marks and fern patterns firm after millennia.

All about Santa Fe the poplars are turning a dry gilt, beautiful still. In *Death Comes for the Archbishop* Willa Cather says they accent this landscape—putting it, as she generally did, with finality. October days are brilliant and warming, with chill nights. The chill gets into the days only late in the month, and by then there is a haziness in the sun, and the Jémez Range is dimmed. By the Pecos River I saw a cedar—I should call it a tall juniper, but out here it's cedar—twined all up through with red woodbine, a gay and Christmasy sight. On another late October day we drove up into the Sangre de Cristos beyond Hyde Park. On the lower road there were still some gold and red-gold groves, but higher, the aspen forest had been stripped and it was like lines of sleet. I noticed the bandage look of the aspen bark. Snow flurries are forecast but there have been none yet.

In mid-October I saw my first pueblo—the greatest of them all, the Taos Pueblo. How strange it seemed under those incredible mountains, with its sacred cottonwood grove, its lively river down the middle, its stark earth. In the recessional masses of its two principal buildings is the true ancestry of American architecture; but as a living place—the ladders from level to level of the houses, the almost deserted quiet of its plaza, the women in their purple shawls coming and going with buckets to the river—as a living place, how foreign it is to us "Americans." Somehow I knew beforehand about the mongrel dogs. And I was both amused and annoyed by a blanketed old Indian who had turned himself into the most persistent walking, talking tourist trap. When at last we bought a clutch of colored corn from him he assured us he was making the price low because we came from Santa Fe.

I have learned a Spanish phrase: *poco a poco*—little by little. It holds the philosophic rhythm of the Spanish-American here, of the Pueblo Indians who were here before him, and, I am beginning to believe, of most of the later invading Anglos.

November

Now the horny toads, sandy-colored on the sand, have scuttled from sight. There are flocks of yellow birds everywhere, like flying toys; or olive-yellow; even an olive hue in the blue of the piñon and sarah jays—somewhat smaller jays than we have in New England. The earth is reddish, dusty, bone-dusty. The sun leaps the Sangre de Cristo Mountains with an immediate morning, and it drops precipitately behind the Jémez Mountains in late afternoon: darkness comes all at once. The gray-green Russian olive trees are beautiful, like tossed veils over the patio walls, and they are loaded now with their fruit. But I am told the olives never mature here, frost comes too early.

The bright afternoons are amazingly comfortable, but the chill at night is much keener. The evening air is fragrant with piñon smoke from all the fireplaces on the Camino. A great deal has been made of this fragrance, but, unless your fireplace isn't operating correctly, you have to go outdoors to enjoy it.

By the second of November there was snow on the peaks of the Sangre de Cristos, a sharp demarcation where the snow line ends. Mornings, the white clouds hover closely, they seem to touch the mountaintops, and the snowcaps appear to smoke into the clouds. On the eleventh, E. and I had cocktails and lunch very comfortably outdoors in Burro Alley. But the next morning clouded early, and the north-northeast quickly thickened a dark gray. Soon the clouds were so deep in the Sangre de Cristos they looked like fog. Obviously it was snowing hard. There was a spit of snow by the house, and the air turned colder. Yet most of this time you could see the Jémez Mountains shining in the sunlight, and the almost clear blue above them. Light leaps such enormous space. In two hours the sun was out again, the mountain peaks new-whitened.

In mid-November I saw my first Indian dances. These were at the Tesuque Pueblo. There were but few of us Anglos watching. And the Indians, absorbed and dignified, paid no attention to us. Their Comanche war dance was brightly costumed and featured feathered headdresses which blew open and shut in the wind. There was the quite tempestuous dancing of the young men and among them, undeviating, the steady pat-pat of the feet of the women. At the end of the line there were a dozen small children tentatively dancing, and there were, ahead of it, the old men beating the drums: there in an eye's containment those who were going to dance and those who had danced. The cries, the banners, added to the exciting and moving rhythms. I was told the dance, though, is but half in earnest. The Comanches were a warlike tribe, terrible raiders of the pueblos; and so adoption of this dance is to an extent a burlesque. I figured the basic beat as ONE-two, ONE-two, ONE-two, ONE-two, ONE-two-two-two, ONE-two-two-two, ONE-two-two-two. That run-on of three light beats to one heavy interested me, since I think the basis of an American poetic line, as differing from English blank verse, would be a preponderance of light accents over the number of heavy.

The deer dance begins in a wonderfully thrilling way. At dawn the costumed men come down out of the hills, slowly, toward the pueblo plaza, each man leaning sharply forward on two short sticks, thus simulating a four-legged creature, and each with his head in antlers. The dance itself is formed of two lines, side by side, and after a few minutes of facing one way the lines turn the other; over and over. It is the turning which is so beautiful, the turning of head and shoulders consecutively through the whole line, making a sort of wave motion. The drums and the heavy downbeat of the dancers' feet, shaking the bells and shells that adorn their legs, build up a powerful rhythm. In theater or out, I have never seen anything more exciting.

For contrast, take Los Alamos.

E. and I drove up there on the twenty-ninth, having with us our friend Hilary Masters from New York and Mr. and Mrs. J. B. Priestley from England. Priestley had been for some weeks in Texas researching the culture of the new-rich oilmen, and his wife—Jacquetta Hawkes—had been in and around Santa Fe for several weeks researching the pueblo cultures. In the process they had, I gathered, considerably revised their notions for the book on which they were collaborating, *Journey Down a Rainbow,* since Priestley had become convinced there is no culture in Texas and his wife, who had anticipated studying a dead culture among the Indians, had concluded it is very much alive.

We had seen Jacquetta Hawkes quite a few times, at our own house and others': she is tall, handsome, remarkably self-possessed, and probably shy. Priestley, stocky and burly, with pipe and pork-pie hat, is in every round inch of him a British Man of Letters. He rolls along, though, like an old sea captain. I had expected a bluntly rude man—and Santa Fe already has a few more stories to add to that legend—but I found him an amusing and charming companion. He is of course a superb essayist, and he talks a constant wit. When we first met over a couple of drinks some days before the Los Alamos trip, we discussed English and American writing and deplored the increasing academicism in both; and I think there and in the materialistics which Priestley excoriates in America, his audience too seldom notes that he does not speak as one come from a superior nation. More than once, voicing some criticism, he took care to say, "Mind you, we have the same sort of thing going on at home."

At any rate, the Priestleys wanted to see Los Alamos, and we rode their celebrated coattails through the director's office, luncheon at the Lodge, sight-seeing the town, and a tea at the house of a scientist whose wife is English. We were not allowed inside the wired-off section, but the Priestleys' purpose was to get the feel of the place. We all thought it was managed by the directors with rather a heavy hand. The school buildings with great sheets of glass looked excellent. Most of the housing seemed hurried, unimaginative, and cramped. Priestley murmured, "Why don't they nick just a little off the bomb—nobody'd notice—and build bigger and better houses?"

A very nice man, Dr. Crew, had us in charge. E. said, "Suppose I wanted to paint my front door red?"

"You'd have to ask the director's permission."

"Suppose I wanted to add a fireplace to my house?"

"You'd have to ask the director."

"Well," said E., "I don't think I'd last here three months."

"Mrs. Scott," said Priestley, "I doubt if you're going to last till three o'clock."

Altogether I think they found the atmosphere depressingly and curiously sterile. "The scientists have been saying for years, 'Give us the world and we'll remake it,'" Priestley whispered to me. "Well, here it is. And isn't it bloody awful!"

December

In more or less recent years Ruth Benedict and Frank Waters and Edmund Wilson and, now, Jacquetta Hawkes have written of the great Shalako dances at Zuni. There is no point in my trying to follow suit. But I cannot let them go unmentioned, they are so tremendous an experience. They are an annual ceremonial, near the first of December, in which six gods bless six new houses in the village. There are other dancers—the clownish mudheads, and so on—but all is dominated by the ten-foot-tall Shalako figures. The huge mask rests on the shoulders of the Zuni. He works its clattering wooden beak by strings. In the dances he runs and swoops with an amazing grace.

These factual matters are not the point. The point is you feel you are in the presence of towering, barbaric gods. Never more so than when they first appear. That is at dusk, across the river from the village. You stand amidst other Anglos at the edge of the village and peer across, barely able to see the gigantic figures as they slowly approach from the hills. Eerie cries sound here and there in the sudden dark, and the bitter cold, which worsens all night, sets in. For an hour or more the Zunis come and go propitiating the Shalako with gifts. The gods stand very near, but the darkness is so thick you cannot see them, only hear, now and again, the clack of wooden beaks. Then with a rush, surrounded by the seemingly pygmy men of the town, they enter it and each goes to a new house. And then you have a cold evening to wait while the Zunis' feasting takes place; the dances, which last till dawn, do not begin until midnight or after.

My friend from Amherst College, Bill Gibson, went with me. It is a long drive west across the state, a flat and tiresome drive. You at last reach Grants, a horrible, mushrooming town which this month is featuring on its Main Street cardboard Santa Clauses carrying bags labeled "Uranium." Then on to Gallup, tumultuous with Navahos, and perhaps another half-hour or more to Zuni. The Navahos—you would think—live in Ford pickup trucks. They swarmed all over Zuni all night. They and the Zunis are much handsomer than the Pueblo Indians along the Rio Grande, who tend to a sexless fattiness. Among the Navahos particularly we noted many majestic men and some quite beautiful women.

We were treated cordially if any attention was paid to us. Bill, strolling ahead of me in the late afternoon, was invited into a house where preliminary ceremonies were taking place. Edmund Wilson, recording his night there, says he felt a hostile air toward Anglo visitors. But Oliver LaFarge tells me this varies; it depends, he says, on what happened the year before: if some visitor was obstreperous or seemed to ridicule the deeply religious dances, resentment would hold over. Which isn't so startling when you consider that no Spanish-American is allowed in Zuni, owing to resentments dating back several hundred years.

Two or three times in the night I weakened enough to wonder if the adventure was worth it: we were so cold despite long underwear, recourse to the heater in the car, cups of coffee, and forbidden nips of our secreted whiskey. Yes, it was worth it; and we stayed on, wandering from house to house, until the first streak of paleness came over the mesa to the east. We were back in Santa Fe by noon.

As to all the Indian dances I have seen, my first reaction is one of awed admiration of their beauty (however monotonous in lengthy doses), of excitement at their chanting, beating, ringing patterns; and, like all serious observers, I have been moved by the thought of the traditions preserved through uncountable centuries. But I find myself wondering how valid those traditions are to young men who have been to Okinawa and back, to Korea and back, who—many of them—leave their pueblos each day to work at Los Alamos. Do they now believe that these dances will raise corn, bring rain, summon snow? If they do not—then we are witnessing a mere imitation of traditions. If they do—well, suppose we transpose this literary admiration of fixed traditions into terms of our own culture, what do we get? Boston, Massachusetts. For which, of course, there is something to be said; always remembering that Henry James, gazing upon Brattle Street in adjacent Cambridge, could not feel that it was passionate. We may, in other words, be admiring the Indians for a changelessness we ourselves cannot achieve and would not really want; and we may, further, be admiring only a make-believe changelessness. I do not know.

Now in late December the accidents of light and shadow continue in the mountains. But the peculiarity of light which I have been most amazed by is the trick of dawn. In great cities the morning light first strikes the tops of tall buildings and then comes down into the streets. Here is something which seems stranger still: before the sun is up over the Sangre de Cristo Mountains I can see leagues of light already on the western land, and as the sun, still itself not visible, rises behind the eastern range, the early light travels toward us across fifty miles from the west.

January

At midmonth we had our first real snow, the mountains gone, the land closeted with storm. It came down with such a furious quickness, three or four inches in a couple of hours, and on till there was about seven inches, very wet, all trees and walls cottoned with it. During the storm robins flocked into the cedars and hundreds of jays wheeled in excitement and lighted in blue rows on all the wires. The snow stayed a day or so. Here the powerful sun makes short work of it. And on the twenty-seventh of the month I saw two violets in bloom by a south wall.

Our house on the Camino del Monte Sol is one of several built in the 1920's by the five young artists who called themselves the *cinco pintores.* Or started in the 1920's; the young men had little money and these adobe houses evolved a room or so at a time over many years. The Camino—there are caminos this and that in town but ours is known as The Camino—is one of the routes of the sight-seeing buses. It runs from Canyon Road, also considered an "arty" sight, to the foothills of the Old Pecos Trail south of Santa Fe. Part of its charm is alleged to be the road itself, unpaved, dusty, corduroy, and, in wet weather, greasy. Its real charm lies in its gated walls, its rambling houses, its great view of the Sangre de Cristos. We are not, except for the mountains, a tourist sight for grandeur: Santa Fe's show places are scattered elsewhere; there are two or three imposing houses along the Camino, but mostly we run from humble to middle size. I know of one painter, one photographer, one sculptor, and a couple of writers now living on this road; the other residents include some trust-funded people, an insurance man, a doctor, a builder of swimming pools, a retired bill collector, a dealer in antiques and real estate, a perfume manufacturer, and a handful of Spanish-Americans, among them Jesus Rios, from whose wood yard at the foot of the Camino we all buy our fireplace piñon. There are now many new "developments" in and around the town, but the Camino is like almost any older Santa Fe street, in that different races and different economic strata are all mixed together. There is a railroad track in Santa Fe, but no right and wrong side of it.

It was the poet Alice Corbin Henderson who years ago changed this road's name from Telephone Hill. She and her painter husband first lived in a little house down the way, but later built a quite large house and a studio across from where we are renting. There have been other appellations. Mary Austin's biographer, Helen Doyle, after a visit here was asked in Albuquerque, "Did you see Nut Row?" Miss Doyle thought she hadn't, but at last discovered her questioner meant the Camino del Monte Sol: "That's it! That's it!—The street where those queer people built all their crazy houses!" And there was also a phrase, "mud-hut nuts."

This bourgeois scorn, I take it, is a thing of the past. The conventional mind is usually also a commercial mind, and it has over recent decades seen something come to pass: the houses these artists built and the pictures they painted were the first teasers of tourist trade, which now has become Santa Fe's greatest industry. So much for the queer, impractical artist!

As a literary fellow, I was first of all interested in the dead. We have by now made an astonishing number of friends, but of course this does not happen overnight and the first two or three months E. and I were much by ourselves; a Spanish girl watched out for the children, and E. and I walked and walked the town. I was interested that the house across the road had been Mrs. Henderson's, that the big brown adobe farther down had been Mrs. Austin's, that the painter John Sloan spent thirty summers in the pink stucco house on Garcia Street, that Willa Cather on a visit here used to stroll up from La Fonda to Mrs. Austin's house to write letters—and of course Miss Cather's great Archbishop's cathedral (and much more of his creation) sits in the center of town. I have discovered that my landlord taught the poet Arthur Davison Ficke woodworking down cellar in this house while Mary Austin sat combing her abundant hair in our little back patio, and that he once painted a portrait of a friend of mine, Bertha Damon (who wrote *Grandma Called It Carnal*), in the one second-story room—accessible by an outside wooden stair—where I work. The girl said to be the original of Brett Ashley in *The Sun Also Rises* used to come to parties in this house—a friend of mine recalls seeing her drain a pint of whiskey in the moonlight on the Camino—and she died of T.B. at the local hospital. And I have met here the man said to be Robert Cohn in the same novel.

Mary Austin has been dead twenty years and her ashes are on top of Cedros Mountain overlooking this canyon. She was the queen of the art colony as the poet Witter Bynner was and still is its prince—and princely host to "everybody" in the world of the arts who passes through. As a college boy back East I once heard Mrs. Austin lecture, and I still remember the piled hair and great comb, and how placidly she announced, "I know more about the

Indians than any other white person." Her ego was large, and I am told she was terribly jealous of *Death Comes for the Archbishop;* at least one of her friends, "out of loyalty to Mary," has refused to read that novel.

February

February afternoons are often soft and easy, but they can turn abruptly into icy cold days and more snow. The chamisa is beginning to change from winter gray-blue to a lizard green.

Early in the month flocks of bluebirds flew everywhere in quick, updrafted flight. It was cold and snowy, but the bluebirds, everybody said, were a sure sign of spring. After a fortnight they were gone—presumably higher, into the mountains.

I play with the notion that birds go into shrubs and trees of colors similar to their own: little yellow and olive-yellow birds into the now yellow-green tamarisk (it is not pink at this season), and gray birds into the cedars. But I must say I also saw yesterday in the cedars a red-headed, yellow-striped woodpecker.

Always in storms and squalls there are those active gatherings of the birds, which I had earlier noted. Sometimes the snow pours straight and quiet as salt from a saltcellar, and then the bluebirds line the wires, the red-bellied robins and the chickadees congregate in the cedars, and there they all sit as at a sort of service.

March

A Chinese student, visiting in Santa Fe, burst into tears on the road between Espanola and Taos and said, "This is China! This is home!" Kenneth Foster of the Museum of Navaho Ceremonial Art says it is like China. The Cyrus Baldridges say: Persia.

Is it also Biblical? There are those who feel so. I suppose it is the mixture of mountains and barren dryness, the occasional river and water hole, the flocks of sheep and herds of goats, the primitive life lived close to a hard earth. Yet E. thinks it is a feminine land—you can toy with equating a lunar landscape to moon to woman to love to death—and she thinks that, so far, women have written of it most perceptively: Cather and Austin and Erna Fergusson. Then there is a consistency, if this feminine theory is true, in the old-womanlike faces of the middle-aged Pueblo Indians; they are stout and appear nonvirile and non-sexual.

This land has been put into some good painting, along of course with a great deal of bad, and it has been documented and described through whole shelves of books. It is not at all as unrecorded as so many Easterners seem to suppose. It has not been seized by poetry—as though perhaps it is too huge and strange. D. H. Lawrence's poems which emanated from here are clusters of images; like too many of his poems they fail the essential question, Why verse? Mrs. Henderson and Witter Bynner have made use of the Indian—Bynner most notably in his "A Dance for Rain"; Haniel Long, also resident here many years, found a natural run of references in the countryside, but Long's most indigenous and remarkable work is of the Spanish invasion, the prose books *Malinche* and *Interlinear to Cabeza de Vaca*.[1] I mean only that no poet has mined, or attempted to mine, this landscape as, for instance, Robinson Jeffers has the West Coast. Jeffers has achieved a lifetime of identification as profound as Robert Frost's with New England or Thomas Hardy's with his Wessex. Is this land too remote for human identification, too anti-human, too perfectly suited as the locale of the most anti-human weapon man has devised? Think of how much of the earth which we can casually gaze up to has probably never felt the tread of man's foot.

Writing of Arizona, Priestley said what may be said in this connection of New Mexico: "If Shakespeare had ever seen such nights of stars, he would have gone mad trying to improve upon his 'Look, how the floor of heaven is thick inlaid with patines of bright gold!' But literature does not like too much encouragement, which is why some of the best lyrical poetry, ecstatic in its praise of nature, has been written by fellows shivering and fogbound in dark attics. No real poetry has come out of Arizona yet, and not much painting. Nature is doing it all."

I have a letter from Henry Beston, who says: "The region is indeed a fantastic one, a lunar one, and to my mind, rather

---

[1]Reissued as the *The Power Within Us*.

dubiously related to any white man. I'm quite sure that the Santa Fe folk who dwell in it, clinging to [the] red man's shirt tail are doing themselves no good. The red man's fancy for reducing everything to the symbol of a symbol was a form of killing . . . A country—like the human being—needs to be born 'of water and the spirit.' Those western places are waterless . . . no life."

This is a point of view once expressed by Lawrence: "But it is without a soul, it has no spirit. It is cold and empty, a landscape of the moon. It has no soul, America has no soul. And it will never have one. It is dead . . . I feel I should die if I had to live here. The whole country, the mountains, the air, it is so hopelessly empty. Even the birds don't sing, it is all dead! It needs to be reborn, to be lived in . . . The Indians, too, are dead. The whole atmosphere stinks of dead bones . . . There is too much menace in the landscape . . . America . . . has a powerful disintegrating influence upon the White psyche. It is full of grinning, un-appeased aboriginal demons, too, ghosts, and it persecutes the White men like some Eumenides, until the White men give up their absolute whiteness. America is tense with latent violence and resistance . . . The American landscape has never been at one with the White man."

Now this is all pitched to the exaggerated misinformation of "Even the birds don't sing." It is Lawrence lashing himself from a small perception to a continental theory, from a New Mexican mountainside to all America. In this mood he didn't want birds singing.

But Lawrence in a famous passage expressed another view: "I think New Mexico was the greatest experience from the outside world that I ever had. It certainly changed me forever. Curious as it may sound, it was New Mexico that liberated me from the present era of civilization, the great era of material and mechanical development . . . The moment I saw the brilliant proud morning shine high up over the deserts of Santa Fe, something stood still in my soul, and I started to attend. There was a certain magnificence in the high-up day, a certain eagle-like royalty . . . for a greatness of beauty I have never experienced anything like New Mexico . . . Just day itself is tremendous there. It is so easy to understand that the Aztecs gave hearts of men to the sun."

Altogether, these people find that the southwestern landscape is overwhelming, that if it belongs to anyone it belongs to the Indian, who is dead; even Lawrence's great paragraph of praise consummates its tone in a note of death.

With Jacquetta Hawkes, I would say the Indian culture is not dead. But I would add that of course it is not for us. There remains the land. The body of poems[2] which has commented, so to speak, upon it is considerable. I am not denigrating all those poems. I am only saying the large possessive grasp of major poetry has not been attempted. Is it more true here than elsewhere that "the land was ours before we were the land's"? If so we are still waiting to belong. It may be that the statement of a great poet, as always reflective of experience and anticipatory to it, would itself lift us into that belonging. And as always, for us fully to realize it, the flesh of the earth must be made word.

"It needs . . . to be lived in."

April

There is one aspect of the Indian culture which fascinates me when looked at in our own terms. This is the Indian sand painting, which has at last been preserved in the Navaho museum here in Santa Fe. There are hundreds of these paintings in beautiful colors and highly stylized symbols. In the museum they have been fixed and kept as art. But that is the white man's doing. What in fact is the Indian sand painting? It was done on the ground inside the dwelling of a physically or mentally ill person. I believe it was always done in series: each day for five or six days a new sand painting replaced that of the day before. In other words, each beautiful work was wiped out.

However, it was not made as a beautiful work. It was not art, it was magic. It was created not for itself but to perform a function—to make someone well.

The white man, regarding all this, is thrown into ambiguous responses. To him it is not magic, but it is art. He cannot help thinking how contradictory its daily destruction is to the average artist's impulse toward permanence. And, after all, the pictures are made with art. Of course their patterns are set and repeated

[2]See *The Turquoise Trail*, edited by Alice Corbin Henderson, 1928.

through long tradition; they are not lost, only removed. All the same, is there anywhere a more vivid illustration of how head-on different our culture is from that of the Indian? All ancient and primitive arts were magic. It is civilized man who has determined that they exist for their own sakes. The profound difference is individualism, scarcely comprehended by the Indian but the very center of our thinking. These sand paintings were a tradition made out of the group for the individual—not the other way round; and the go-between, the man who reproduced the magic, had no aesthetic importance.

Yet here I must mention a man named George Coluzzi. He was an artist. He was from Boston and it was presumed he was rich, for he gave away a lot of money and he himself lived shabbily—at one time, by choice, in a cave on the edge of Santa Fe. He also lived so thoroughly dirty that when his cat scratched him he became at once infected and died. All this was a decade or so back. But the thing I have heard about Coluzzi which charms me no end is this: A powerful man, Coluzzi now and then would lug huge rocks down from the hills, sculpt them, and then return them to where he had found them.

It is rumored that one or more of these have been come upon and identified as prehistoric.

May

April was the windiest month, and we had dust storms out of the dead land. The days warmed. The one lovely event was the blossoming of the fruit trees, everywhere; first the apricot, then the cherry and peach and pear coming on. Here the fragility of spring blossoming is italicized, since it takes place against heavy adobe walls and the rugged countryside. We are running a month behind on weather, I am told. March, not April, should have been dusty, and lilacs, usually out in April, have bloomed in mid-May. Even in New England I have never seen such abundance of lilacs. All Santa Fe seems one massive bush of white and purple. Circles, rows, hedges of them—they are all over town. And there is a knee-high lilac which blooms right along with the big ones. We have had some soaking rains in the city and there is still snow on the Sangre de Cristo Mountains. In town, the white seed of the cottonwood drifts in the grass like snow.

June

I disapprove of cemeteries and I like them. I believe they are sentimental and unnecessary and I should hate to be without them. Of course I am thinking in terms—or rather, feeling in terms—which I am used to, that is in terms of New England; of tree-shaded peace or even, for it has its charm, the hot and deep-grassed neglect of the oldest of God's acres. There is in Santa Fe an Anglo attempt to reproduce that grassed and shaded cemetery, and at Taos, in the little cemetery where Kit Carson is buried, there is a naturally wooded area which is pleasant. But most of the cemeteries out here are ghastly.

Indian graves you seldom see, for Indian burial is almost always a secret obliteration. It is the Spanish-American grave-yards that have so depressed me. They are topsy-turvy with crazy crosses, names fading, artificial flowers faded, and all a weedy desolation. Nothing is tended, nothing there is meant to last. It is this landscape again: a man hardly makes a gesture—he knows it would be such a foolish gesture—to defy it.

Yet the painter Agnes Tait notes a human contribution. Speaking the other day of a natural orderliness in the landscape, its level sagebrush, its inevitable flow to the mountains and upward, she said man contributes by neatness: he is poor—he picks up and saves.

Spectacular as this country is, as with any other, you become accustomed to it. I don't mean it could as well be the plains of Kansas, for light and the seasons are always busy arranging its heights and depths; but you get familiar even with that. Still—if you go away a little while and return, there is the awed wonder fresh again; or if in a sense you look consciously after some days of disregard, you catch a new drama. As, even now, I have been watching the tide of green advancing day to day up the mountain slopes.

And sometimes, as anywhere, you see it all anew because somebody is newly arrived with whom you see it. The other afternoon I stood in front of the Folk Art Museum at the south edge of town with William Carlos Williams. We gazed out across the piñon-pocked foothills flounced with green cottonwoods and "accented" by poplars in the seemingly arrested sunlight. He said, "It looks like eternity."

July

Presumably aside from any jealousy she may have felt for Willa Cather's intrusive achievement in *Death Comes for the Archbishop,* Mary Austin regretted Miss Cather's implied admiration for the Archbishop's French cathedral. "It was a calamity to the local culture," said Mrs. Austin. She was right. It does not belong here. But pioneers customarily hark back to their own building traditions before they go on to evolve or discover what is proper to their new country; and that precisely is what Archbishop Lamy did.

In the 1920's, when Santa Fe was still a small town and the Anglos were still a minority, "It was always," says Bynner, "Palace Avenue against the Camino." Palace Avenue, running east from the plaza, is an Anglo street of bungalows and a few imposing houses echoing the General Grant era; it has some of the homely little brick cottages, scattered all over town, which are the remnants of a time when the U.S. Army maintained a base here. But of course the "mud-hut nuts" on the Camino del Monte Sol were not doing the odd and strange thing at all as they piled up their adobe houses and roofed them with dirt, stones, and anything else that was handy and looked durable. Those artists were revivalists of an architecture and in their radicalism were quite as traditional as your New England builder of "Colonial." At the present time, by the way, any new building or any doing over occurring on Palace Avenue usually simulates the adobe style. The "mud-hut nuts" have long since triumphed.

Actually there are two types of architecture that suit this land—always excepting what would seem to be splendid possibilities here of "modern," if the overwhelming quantity of sun is correctly handled. The other is called Territorial Style. It is a chaste and more formal building, usually with stucco walls and capped all along the roof line with brick. It is used domestically and has been handsomely adapted for large public buildings, notably the Capitol in Santa Fe. And it is, of all things, yet another version of the Greek Revival.

The adobe remains the more indigenous and it has been used from the Indian pueblos, the humblest Spanish-American compounds, to houses built by wealthy Anglos that can fetch between fifty and a hundred thousand dollars. The largest all-adobe building in the world is the great Cristo Rey Church on Canyon Road, a church that would have pleased Mary Austin. Significantly it features a magnificent stone reredos salvaged from a dark room downtown where it had been jammed away as inappropriate in Archbishop Lamy's Romanesque cathedral.

I have found myself reminded of Bermuda. Either way, it's a far cry from Bermuda to Santa Fe. Yet here, as there, a beautifully natural architecture has, as it were, been excavated. Here as there the housing materials have been dug out of the ground and set together by hand and the result is an architecture which seems to have been forced by the land itself. Here too, though most often the adobe house is a brown or tan color on the overlay of plaster or stucco, pastel shades of pink and blue are frequently used. Doors and window trim are often painted blue or turquoise.

It is an admirable architecture and, first of all, it passes the test of functionalism. The thick adobe wall gives first-rate insulation, warm in winter and cool in summer. It will take easily, as New England "Colonial" will not, the modern large window. In all sizes it has a massive feel to it. Yet it is so malleable that you hardly have a true line anywhere: windows and fireplaces are rounded, corners are rounded, the walls lean a little inward or outward: it makes a flowing continuation of grace and mass. It is almost always a one-story architecture, and the roof is supported by round logs—*vigas*—which dramatize the ceiling. The interior walls are usually painted white.

What amazes the visitor is, first, that though most adobe houses "don't look like much" from the outside, one after another is a superbly comfortable and colorful house. This occurs in part because adobe housing includes the walled patio, and you get little idea from the road what is going on in room and garden. I have a theory that the land again—the immensity of land—dictates the walled-in tradition: man has to be able to enclose himself to feel a sense of security amidst spaces too vast for him to cope with. And, second, the visitor is amazed by the variety within the form: no two houses are ever quite alike and they are very often much unlike.

Now the sad truth is that the primitive block of mud and straw has become an expensive labor in building, and true adobe houses are rarely made. We are into the era of the fake. Cinder block and two-by-fours go up in the "developments," and the architecture, as the old crack has it, "is put on afterward." This is the conventional pattern, all the way from the fake "Colonial" house in New England to the steel-girdered "Gothic" cathedral in New York. And, as always, the fakery shows—in substitution of repetitive conformity for imaginative creation, in a machine-cut look, in a less functional housing. Fakery is always a substitution of *seem* for *be;* it won't do for poetry, as MacLeish long since observed; and indeed it won't do for anything. Fortunately the true essence of Santa Fe is as authentic as the hills around us.

August

I am aware that I have written of landscape with few figures. I have wanted to record a sense—while mine was still fresh—of place. I have not wanted at this time to write of the many people who have come and gone or come and stayed in our life during this year. Yet, though I cannot turn economist or sociologist, I am sure it is necessary to suggest at least the sense of society if one is going to bring together all those suggestions of that sense of place. There is, as I said at the beginning, magic in the land. But there are mountains elsewhere, and green valleys of trees and fields, and desert places. Landscape of itself is never enough for man.

Well, I can do no better than steal a paragraph from Paul Horgan's *The Centuries of Santa Fe.* He says: "It was always difficult to fix upon the particular stimulus amid all the general charms which had most to do with bringing modern colonists to town. Some spoke of the altitude, with its bracing effect; others of the air, the light, the color all about. Yet beyond these something else could be felt. It was an insinuation of freedom in behavior, not in any publicly unsavory terms, but rather in an opportunity for an individual man or woman to live a life of free expression. In modern times, was this the most significant—and perhaps the most Latin—of attractions about Santa Fe?"

It is not a society free of criticism. Yet we have found, for our own part, a wide intermingling without regard to sexual proclivities or age or economic status: all three on exhibit here in every conceivable variety. Whatever your interests may be, Santa Fe provides many companions in them, and nowhere we have ever lived has there been this in such abundance nor has there been so easy a coming and going among one's own kind; and one's own kind cross all those lines of sex, age, and money.

Here the artist can be, as Mr. Horgan says, "accounted," and in how many places, he asks, is that true? And the artist is accounted without pressures. May Sarton, the poet and novelist, is a frequent visitor, and I thought she put it well when she said, "Here you can say you're a writer and they say, 'Fine!' They don't say, 'Who's your agent? When's your new book coming out?' "

It is unavoidable that the significant attraction of Santa Fe brings in the escapee, the malcontent, the failure, the exhibitionist, the dubiously talented. Outsiders sometimes consider the place to be "full of frauds." It is not. There are many genuinely talented people who work steadily and quietly right along with the keepers of grocery stores and the ambitious young exploiters of uranium. Santa Fe is not an artists' colony; it is predominantly a workaday city with a full share of the kind of man Dorothy Parker once pined for—the kind "who solicits insurance." Its only disproportion seems to me to be in the delightful number of beautiful women from fifteen to seventy-five. Walking through town is a sexual experience. For so small a city there is a surprising variety of groups; you think you have met everybody, but you haven't—there are other circles spinning in their own orbits. But there is tolerance away beyond the average, a live-and-let-live which Paul Horgan has so exactly put his finger upon.

I can speak only as an Anglo, and one still inexpert even of my own race. Between the Indians and the Spanish-Americans there is some but very little intermingling. Ourselves, we go to the Indians' places as witnesses of strangeness; they come to us with things to sell. Perhaps they despise us. Who could blame them? Of course there are individual relationships, as there are between the Spanish and ourselves. There is cordiality between the ancient and the new invaders; again, I think it is mostly specific, not general. They call us, behind our backs, "gringos," and we get apprehensive about their knife-carrying, street-roving adolescents, their "pachucos." Still, there is rarely real trouble. Racial and religious differences are not morbid. We are desegregated and I should surmise the relationships between the races are continually easing. Here, as anywhere in the world, it is a matter of education. Along with streaks of childlike wildness, there is a great gentleness in the Spanish-Americans; if they are more often shiftless than we, they are often kinder. Their slow talk and easy rhythm of life are an integral part of the essence here. It is all *poco a poco.*

You could live a cocktail-party existence here; some do. For my kind of person it can be an overstimulating place—your head next morning is filled with too much conversation, too much personality of others vibrant with that freedom of behavior. Distraction is a danger. And there are those—Robinson Jeffers, as a visitor, among them—who have told me that they find the atmosphere here conducive to pleasant coma but not to work. But many of us have reacted differently.

So many of us are immigrants, whether of a quarter-century or more ago or of a year ago, that I think we are self-conscious about Santa Fe and too filled with defenses. We are converts. To make a choice is to assume a defensive position. At least at first. "Where did you come from? What made you decide to stay here?" We are constant in that conversation. Whole rooms of people can get happily smug on it, as though it were an opium of self-congratulation. It is, I think, something to outgrow. We have a local columnist who seldom reports a more or less newsworthy tourist without concluding that he or she was so enchanted as to hope to return here forever. It can't always be so. And who wants everybody here? Or even "everybody"? As Dr. Fromm long since reminded us, most people try to escape from freedom.

September again

—and this is where we came in a year ago, for a year. The surging rhythms of this land into which we so incautiously stepped are now beginning to repeat their round. The air is thinning bluer. On all the roads and foothills the chamisa is turning gold again. Downtown the annual fiesta is in full cry: booths around the plaza dispensing hot dogs and circus candy and clutter; parades both religious and for fun; La Fonda jammed with the liquorous. I find myself thinking: I'll be glad when this is all over and the *turistas* have departed and we have our town back again all nice and quiet. And I smile at myself as I think it.

A year ago, on all sides, we were told, Of course you'll never go back. We were told, If you go back you won't be satisfied, and then you'll return for good. But we have made our decision without returning. I shall go back only after I have really settled.

There are many people here from back East. Of course people from Detroit think they are from back East. But I mean, literally, many long-rooted New Englanders like me. Sometimes when some of us are together we indulge in those smug conversations I have mentioned. Sometimes we speak of the sea.

8

The Unrelenting Land

JOHN DeWITT McKEE

John DeWitt McKee is professor of English at the New Mexico
Institute of Mining and Technology, Socorro, New Mexico, and author
of Two Legs to Stand On *(1955).*

New Mexico answers no questions. It is as impersonal as an equation, as unpersonified as a law of physics, and more immutable. Yet not immutable at all, but ever-changing; set solid as a boulder, yet changing with the sun. The land itself sings no songs, tells no tales, will not be romanticized into prettiness. It does not give, nor does it ask.

Still we stand fascinated by the unanswered question, pulled like Ulysses to the unsung song, stretched tight to breaking toward the story that quivers forever on the brink of being. And if we are tuned, we vibrate to the unheard melody, we take the salt of wisdom from the words unspoken.

What is it then that holds us to this curious, raw, new, old and savage land? It is not love, for the land itself is too aloof for love. It is not landscape, for there is no landscape here. There is only the land, which can no more be trapped for taming than can the fleeting watermelon color of the mountains, come and gone between one eye-blink and the next. Landscapes can be whistled in and brought to heel, ordered and arranged in frames. But this!

Reprinted from the *New Mexico Quarterly* 27, no. 3 (Autumn 1957) by permission of the author.

So seemingly inert, impassive, barren, this land will not submit to capture.

The land's alive. It has a tensile strength unknown in the matronly luxuriance of greener places. It has a thrusting power not found in the contented pregnancy of midland fields. This land is impassive, yes; but it is never passive. The land itself by slow degrees takes those who come to it and shapes them till they fit, till they take the color of the desert, till they can look almost unwaveringly at the sky. This is the land then. This it is that holds us, this and the paradox.

Consider the paradox. Here is a land uncompromising in its honesty, the naked geologic ribs of earth stripped for man to try to conquer. There is about this land an unrelenting clarity whose very air would seem to make a lie impossible.

Nevertheless, a shabby falseness walks upon this land, a movie-set unreality which stems, perhaps, from insecurity and results in an intellectually self-conscious insistence that the observer take for bed-rock reality what is instead either imported veneer or artificial and mechanical resurrection.

For the culture that exists here—as opposed to the Culture which is so hopefully advertised—is a colloidal compound of traditions. Some of the traditions were here from the beginning; they grew from the earth with the Indian. Some came from Spain or Mexico, some from the Midwest, some from the South, others from New England. This land, which is like a cat and belongs to no man, has taken to itself the traditions of all of Western man. There is no culture here. There are only cultures, swirled together like many oils of different weights, on water.

What stands for culture here, however, makes much of Culture. It shows off like a boy walking a board fence. It takes inordinate pride in its success in blending "three cultures," by which it means the Indian, the Spanish, and every other culture of which the New Mexican is compounded, which it lumps as "Anglo."

As for blending, we've taken the architecture of the Pueblo Indian, which grew out of earth and necessity and remained a part of the land, and we've built things of steel and hollow tile and cement blocks, adding useless mass because that mass is a part of the appearance of Pueblo architecture, and we've called it

72

"modified Pueblo." We've hung dubious Navajo blankets in front of roadside "snake pits" to draw the tourist trade, and we've provided places where you can "watch the Indians work," like queer fish in a waterless aquarium, while they make for you "authentic" Indian jewelry.

Here society seems somehow transplanted, too—like an orchid in the desert—unreal, pretentious, self-conscious. Adolescent Albuquerque, the biggest city in New Mexico, its nerve center, its cultural hub, goes into the world of after-dark wearing green mascara and falsies and sophistication.

Here individuality has become a cult, demanding a sort of conformity in non-conformity. There is pride in being an artistic center, a literary center, a meeting place for intellectuals. But it is a defensive pride. New Mexico is not unique in this. It is, in fact, a national phenomenon which began in colonial days. But the poseur is the more obvious because the works of man, dabbed impertinently upon the face of agelessness, ephemeral everywhere, seem even more so here.

The organized individualists decry the decline of taste, and write and paint and think in circles, to be read and viewed and discussed in the closed circle of the organization, creating a sort of artistic and intellectual hoop snake with its tail in its mouth. Nothing can succeed, apparently, unless it is organized. One must "belong" to dance the square dance, to grow a beard, to appreciate poetry, to love horses, or to learn to unsex the Chinese elm. Recreation itself is organized and departmentalized and loaded with people who have been especially trained to organize it and departmentalize it.

Neither is this a provincial nor a regional matter. It is nationwide, and it goes beyond the arts and recreation. The plumbers, the morticians, the service station attendants, the bakers, the bottlers, the meat packers, the dry cleaners, the model builders, the philatelists, the hi-fi addicts—name your group. It *is* a group, complete with president, vice president, secretary and treasurer.

Perhaps no man can any longer face the immensity and complexity of the land alone. Perhaps the idea of "teamwork"—in medicine, in advertising, in religion, in nearly every human endeavor—is a necessary weapon with which to combat fear. And perhaps the very insistence on organization has generated a fear of being alone. If the soul needs solitude as the tree needs room to grow, we may be afraid to grow. For even if we pride ourselves on being different, we surround ourselves, for protection, with others who are being different in like manner.

The group is everywhere, but here it is more obvious, being naked. Against this land, beneath this sky, men gather under banners to give necessary meaning to themselves. Much is made of diversity, and there is diversity in plenty. But it is group, not individual, diversity. It is self-conscious diversity, supported by organization for its own sake. It does not have the integrity that makes differentness incidental. Only from an honest and unpretentious expression of self can grow, paradoxically, a fundamental unity. And from that unity can grow a culture that fits like a loose jacket, with no necessity to call attention to itself. The culture here, on the other hand, binds the swelling chest of its own self-consciousness.

There is a reason for this, too. American society has always been fluid, always moving, always looking for the new frontier. And here is the last of the frontiers. This land which is old is yet so new. What was a somnolent village yesterday may be a bursting city today, with the stink of boom about it. There is space to move here. The new frontiersmen see the space, the sky and the mesa, the desert and the forest, but they are baffled by the land that under-girds them. Or they ignore it.

The artist deprecates, and is deprecated by, the businessman; the scientist jostles the cattleman; the intellectual shouts baffled imprecations from his tower; and the features of the Indian become more and more blurred as he becomes more and more "assimilated" and helps the white man carry his burden. The dances, the legends, the art, and the religion of the Indian are already being mummified and preserved in the collection cases of the "tradition" hunters.

And here they place a tradition in an iron lung and will not let it die a decent death. They build an association around it to give pneumatic similitude of life to the tradition, and busyness to minds besieged by boredom. They do not realize that when it is pumped up and preserved in associations and annual meetings, it is as false as the seeming blush of life on the rouged face of a corpse. They fail to see, for instance, that the strength of aesthetic pleasure in folk arts is rooted in the absolute material and spiritual necessity of those arts. They do not realize, for example, that the conglomeration which passes for Spanish Colonial or modified Pueblo, because it is cut off from the roots of aesthetic and pragmatic necessity, is bastard architecture. The fiesta dress, on the other hand, is in a tradition and is alive. It is alive because it is aesthetically pleasing, and it is practical. So far as architecture is concerned, a new tradition may arise in the Southwest out of the growing practicality of solar heating. These things can become and remain traditions because they grow out of the needs of the people on the land and out of the land itself.

It is fascinating, this New Mexico, and the paradox is no less fascinating than the land. But one can only explore. New Mexico gives no answers. It is a grinding, clashing, many-cornered conglomerate. It is cattle and oil and cotton; it is mines and pines and mountains. It has, in spite of all the unconscious attempts to spoil it, a fine, firm honesty, like the uncompromising, harsh beauty of the malpais. But it wears a coy curtain of posing, poster-paint culture, much like the flapping canvas come-on of a carnival sideshow. The backdrop is real; the show itself is not; for behind the curtain is still the same hula girl from Keokuk.

Yet the land holds us and shoves our roots hard and deep into the rock beneath the shifting sand. The sky holds us, curved tight about the land like the blue bubble of a bomber. And the scything wind-sweeps of the cattle-dotted grasslands; the dust-blown, curving plow tracks in the cotton fields in winter, and the nodding, waving whiteness of the same fields in the fall; the oil pumps, singly or in ranks, sucking nectar from the earth like metal mantises, living to devour—these hold us and mark this place as home. Rising out of long forgotten seas like a massive shrug of shoulders, the mountains stand firm and hold us. Volcanic cones against the sky, monuments to the grandeur of past violence, hold us, too, in something that approaches awe.

Man may scratch the past with his frail stick plow. He may fling himself into the future seeking limits to the limitless sky. He may strut upon a stage too vast for any drama he may make or comprehend. It does not matter. It is the land that holds us here. It is the unrelenting land, this great, fierce, challenging, canyon-gutted, mesa-muscled land, which holds us and which gives us space enough to write a life on—and leaves it to us whether we have courage enough and faith to fill the page.

9

"Why Albuquerque?"

ERNIE PYLE

*Ernie Pyle (1900–1945) won the Pulitzer Prize in 1944 for his
distinguished war correspondence. The "dirt street" in front of the
Albuquerque home described here is Girard Boulevard.*

People all over the country are always saying to me: "You
travel constantly and have been all over America and have seen
all the nice places to live, so you choose Albuquerque out of the
whole United States. Why Albuquerque?"

Well, that's a hard question to answer. There are many little
reasons, of course. But probably the main thing is simply a deep,
unreasoning affection for the Southwest.

I guess it's like being in love with a woman. You don't love a
woman because she wears No. 3 shoes or eats left-handed or has a
diamond set in her front tooth. You just love her because you love
her and you can't help yourself. That's the way we are about the
Southwest.

I was born and raised in the farm country of Indiana. "That
Girl"—who is Mrs. Pyle—came from among the lakes and trees of
lovely Minnesota. But we both adjourned to the East, and lived
and worked in Washington and New York most of our adult
lives.

But finally two pairs of itching feet combined to send us on our
way, into what is probably the freakiest newspaper job in

America. We just simply wander constantly around, and write a daily column about it for the Scripps-Howard Newspapers, and many others too.

When we left Washington seven years ago, we stored our scant possessions in a warehouse. For the next six years we were without a home or even a base, of any sort. We lived constantly in hotels or on boats; we took our vacations wherever we happened to be; we have been sick in hotel rooms all the way from Alaska to Santiago, Chile; we had clothes and books and suitcases cached away in the homes of friends clear from Los Angeles to New York.

We do like this gypsy life. It frees you of a great many responsibilities. You can always pay your bill and run on to some other place before events catch up with you. You are free in a way that isn't possible to a permanent resident. Gypsying is in our blood, and even today after 250,000 miles of going-away-from-where-we-are, we still couldn't bear to think of settling down permanently.

And yet, as the years of wandering rolled over us, we began to sense a lack of something. We realized we had become human whirling dervishes. We had become footloose finally to the point of just swinging forever through space without ever coming down. We were like trees growing in the sky, without roots.

So at last we decided to acquire a base. Not for the purpose of settling down, not a permanent hearthside at all, but just some definite walls in a definite place that we could feel were ours. A sort of home plate, that we could run to on occasion, and then run away from again.

Now we had first seen the Southwest way back in 1926, when we came through in a Model-T Ford roadster on a crazy kid tour of America. We had loved it at that first sight. Then in these more recent years of traveling we had hit the Southwest—as we did almost all other parts of the nation—at least once a year. We became better and better acquainted with the desert country, we made personal friends, there grew in us an overwhelming warmth of feeling for the uncanny sweeps of empty space in this part of the world. And thus it was that when in late 1940 we decided to build this so-called base somewhere in America, we didn't even have to take a vote on where it should be. We just decided by acclamation. We had never discussed it before, but we both knew without asking. The place was New Mexico.

Under our original plans we would have been in this house only one month of each year—while we took our annual vacation. But circumstances stepped in and took a hand. The war, and sickness, and other events shaped our course until in this past year, we have spent four months in our new house in Albuquerque, instead of one. For the first time in our lives we have become householders. We haven't stopped traveling, and we don't think of ourselves as living permanently even in our own home—but in these four months we have got pretty well acquainted with this little center of the universe that we retreat to. And we are not sorry we built our base in Albuquerque.

By the time this appears in print I will again be far away. But the house will be here for us to come back to. And all the things we like about being in Albuquerque will be here when we return. And here are the things we like about living in Albuquerque:

We like it because we have a country mailbox instead of a slot in the door. We like it because our front yard stretches as far as you can see, and because old Mt. Taylor, 65 miles away, is like a framed picture in our front window. We like it because when we look to the westward we look clear over and above the city of Albuquerque and on beyond, it seems, half way to the Pacific Ocean.

We like it because you can cash a check almost anywhere in Albuquerque without being grilled as though you were a criminal. And because after your second trip to a filling station the gas-pumper calls you by name.

We like it because people are friendly and interested in you, and yet they leave you alone. To a vain fellow like me, it is pleasant to be stopped on the streets downtown by perfect strangers and told they enjoy your column; and yet these thoughtful strangers do not ask anything of you and do not keep you standing in fretfulness. People in Albuquerque realize that our life and work is one of seeing thousands and thousands of people a year all over the world, and that when we come home to Albuquerque to rest, we do want to see a few people, but not thousands. And so they are considerate of us.

And we like it here because you can do almost anything you

want to, within reason. In four months, I haven't been out of overalls more than half a dozen times. And I go to the Alvarado Hotel's swell *Cocina Cantina* always in my overalls, and nobody raises an eyebrow.

We like it because we can have Navajo rugs in our house, and piñon and juniper bushes in our yard, and western pictures on our knotty-pine walls. We like it because you can take a Sunday afternoon spin into the mountains and see deer and wild turkey; and because I have a workbench where I make crude little end-tables and such stuff for our house.

We like it because you aren't constantly covered with smoke and soot, and because the days are warm and the nights are cool, and because the weirdest kinds of desert weeds are always springing up in our bare south lot. We like it because we can see scores of miles in any direction from our house, and yet we can drive downtown in seven minutes.

We like it because the meadow larks hidden in the sage across the road from our house sing us awake in the summer dawn. The meadow larks sing the oddest things. One of them says over and over "Your face is awfully pretty!" And another one says "Here comes the preacher."

Every night around 9 two rabbits come to nibble on our lawn. And about once a week when we rise early, there are quail in our front yard. We have actually counted as many as 50. And when we go out onto the porch they don't fly away with a frightened whirring of wings, they just walk slowly across the road and inside the concealing sage as though to say "Don't get it into your head we'd leave if we didn't want to. We were through anyway."

We like it out here because we seem to go to bed early and get up early—and certainly out here he who does not see the dawn at least once a week is missing perhaps the loveliest thing the desert has in its Horn of Plenty. We have seen sunrises so violently beautiful they were almost frightening, and I'm only sorry I can't capture the sunsets and the thunderstorms and the first snows on the Sandias, and take them East and flaunt them in people's faces.

We like it here because no more than half our friends who write us know how to spell Albuquerque. We like it here because there aren't any street cars, and because you see lots of men on

Central Avenue in cowboy boots. We like it because you can see Indians making silver jewelry, and you can see sheepskins lying over a vacant downtown lot, drying in the sun. And we like it because the dirt street in front of our house washes into such deep gullies that not many people care to drive over it.

We like it because Albuquerque is still small enough that you always see somebody you know when you go downtown. We like it because the whole tempo of life is slower than in the big cities. We like it because in Albuquerque a pedestrian waits for the traffic light even though there may not be a car in sight.

We like Albuquerque because, in spite of the great comfortable sense of isolation you feel here, still you do not suffer from over-isolation. For people here, too, live lives that are complete and full. We want for little, even in the nebulous realm of the mind. There is no famine of thought in our surroundings. In the Southwest character there is a sufficiency which, though not complacent, has in it something of the desert's charm.

We like it here because you buy gnarled cedar firewood by the pound or ton and people never heard of a "cord." And we like it because you can drive half-an-hour from home and buy a burro for $5—in case you want a burro.

We like it here because we're on top of the world, in a way; and because we are not stifled and smothered and hemmed in by buildings and trees and traffic and people. We like it because the sky is so bright and you can see so much of it. And because out here you actually see the clouds and the stars and the storms, instead of just reading about them in the newspapers. They become a genuine part of your daily life, and half the entire horizon is yours in one glance just for the looking, and the distance sort of gets into your soul and makes you feel that you too are big inside.

Yes, there are lots of nice places in the world. I could live with considerable pleasure in the Pacific Northwest, or in New England, or on the Mississippi Gulf Coast, or in Key West or California or Honolulu. But there is only one of me, and I can't live in all those places. So if we can have only one house—and that's all we want—then it has to be in New Mexico, and preferably right at the edge of Albuquerque where it is now.

10

Old Town and New

HARVEY FERGUSSON

Harvey Fergusson (1890–1971), a native of Albuquerque, was a distinguished novelist, journalist, and scriptwriter.

New Mexico towns, like other desert plants, tend to reach a certain modest size and then grow very slowly if at all. Taos is a place of inextinguishable vitality but it is about the same size now that it was when Kit Carson got there. Santa Fe has gained about two thousand people in two hundred years. Socorro, which boomed on silver, is only a fraction of its former self. Only Albuquerque and a few towns in the eastern part of the state, which rightfully belong to Texas, have grown substantially.

For dreams of wealth this country has surely been a graveyard. The drama of the seven golden cities has been enacted again and again. As Coronado followed a dream of unlimited gold and came away without even his coat of mail, so many another man has lost his shirt seeking wealth along the Rio Grande. The Southwest is perhaps the one large region in the United States where the great American dream of change and progress has most strikingly failed to come true. Here the persistence of primitive stocks and folkways has resisted social change as rock and sun have resisted the plow.

This finally has come to be its chief distinction—that here alone change has not wholly obliterated all that went before, that the past is present in patterns of life and types of men, that the face of the earth is not much altered. It remains, as it has always been, a place of destination, but most of those who come here now come seeking an elusive something they call color or atmosphere or romance or tradition. Whatever you call it, it is inadequately named and means many things to many persons but it surely represents some kind of a genuine need and value.

A man, to be whole, must not live too fast to think. He must reflect much upon his experience, accepting the worst of it, appreciating the best of it, making it all a part of his being, so that each moment is but the focal point of a long clear perspective. If he is too busy and if circumstance is too exigent he loses all sense of continuity, his life lacks significance. And surely it is not otherwise with peoples and nations. America in general has been too busy and the circumstance of change has been overwhelming. Chicago is not a plant with roots in the soil but a huge fungus of machinery and men, and it is a fair sample of industrial America.

A feeling of continuity in our experience as a people, a sense of the past as a living reality conditioning the present are what we have lost. I think even casual observers in New Mexico are aware of a richer and more living background, but to most of them it appears remote and irrelevant to the rest of America. They have dubbed it quaint, strange and picturesque and painted its costume rather than its soul. It is to many a place of romantic escape and they seem to look for the exotic rather than the significant. It has never seemed either strange or a place of escape to me, doubtless in large part because I was born there, but I think it is more intimately integrated with the whole American experience than most Americans know.

The latest invasion of this much invaded land has been an influx of painters and writers and of all those various types of men and women who are the camp followers of every cultural movement. This westward migration of the men with paint and ink on their fingers has given New Mexico a new type of society and a new spurt of life, just as the coming of the beaver trappers and the wagon traders did. It is a part of the region's social history, too important to be overlooked and too recent to be clearly seen.

Taos and Santa Fe now are art colonies whose life is shaped and colored perhaps more by the artists and intellectuals than by any other class. This, I think, is the distinctive thing about them. Santa Fe now has much in common with Greenwich Village, Carmel, Provincetown and all those other foci of cultural infection which pimple the fair face of our land. Not only the same types but many of the same persons are found in all of them.

In America the intellectuals tend to be the most exclusive and self-conscious class in the social aggregation. They tend to live in groups apart, consorting only with each other. The intolerance which they deplore in others is in them often exaggerated to the point of phobia. Doubtless this is inevitable in a country where the fine arts long have borne a measure of disesteem, where the social pressure has been toward material and practical accomplishment, where the life of the mind is traditionally suspect. Doubtless it is also regrettable, for surely the artist should leaven the social lump, should be a man among men of all kinds both for his own good and for theirs.

In New Mexico the painters and writers seem to be more a part of the society they have invaded than anywhere else I have been. They were drawn there in the first place by some felt affinity for the rich primitive background of the place. They have tried to make common cause with the Indians and Mexicans and if the alliance has not resulted in complete mutual understanding it has nevertheless been a genuine and fruitful social contact. Finding the Indians in danger of starvation because they were being robbed of their lands and in danger of losing their identity because of the government policy to make them over into good American farmers, the invading aesthetes have championed the red man. They have flooded the country with literature about their wrongs, have helped to force bills through congress and have caused senators and congressmen to engage in solemn and bewildered investigation of the aboriginal soul. This movement has been rich in absurdity and slow in result but I think it can fairly be said that the aesthetic group in New Mexico has created in the American public a new appreciation of the Indian as a unique and valuable survival who ought to be cherished for what he is rather than made over into something else. I think his extinction as a type of man has been postponed if not prevented.

Here too the painters and writers have more of a genuine and working relationship to the community life as a whole than elsewhere, chiefly because that community as a social organism is relatively small and weak. The literary group that gathered in Chicago a few years ago was widely advertised as a great cultural renaissance which was to move the literary capital of America across the Mississippi. But Chicago as a whole was no more aware of this spiritual phenomenon than a dog is aware of a flea which is not biting him. One by one the cornbelt poets migrated to Manhattan leaving Chicago to Al Capone and Big Bill.

Santa Fe and Taos were incapable of such magnificent ignorance. The artists have brought new life to both places. They have been followed by a troop of tourists with money in their pockets. They have boosted rents and bettered business. They are regarded with a tolerance which may have begun as no more than an appreciation of their cash value but has often grown into something more personal. I think this is one of the few places in America, if not the only one, where poets and painters have become prominent citizens, where hotels and other public places are decorated with the products of local artists and where the architecture of postoffices and movie theaters, as well as of residences, has been influenced by the artists of the community. The plaza in Santa Fe has been almost made over in the Pueblo-Mexican style and it is a daring soul who builds a house in Taos in any other mode. In summary, the artists here have become in some measure a part of society, have quickened the community life and produced a visible and physical effect upon it.

Even Albuquerque, the stronghold of prosperity and progress, the best business town between Pueblo and El Paso, the home of Rotary and Kiwanis, the obedient child of the railroad, has felt the renaissance a little. Recently an old adobe building in Old Albuquerque was made over, not to look like the first national bank, but to look as it had a hundred years ago. With a grand ball it was opened to the public as Albuquerque's Art Center. Here artists were to live and paint—at least so it was hoped and said.

There have never been many artists in Albuquerque but the town at least offered them a home, as one might build a nest box in a tree to lure shy birds.

The opening ball was a costume ball and it was a great success. The daughter of an old Mexican family appeared in a ponderous wedding dress which had been worn in that same house half a century before. A promising young real estate man looked enough like an aboriginal Navajo to tempt the trigger finger of an unreconstructed pioneer. Buffalo Bill was there and Montezuma and more youths in tight Spanish trousers and girls in high Spanish combs than the floor would hold. This town, which has so long lived in its future, now for the first time shows a quickening awareness of its past.

When one turns from the long study of vanished types and cultures to survey the present, he enters a narrow and perilous place, where exaggeration threatens and speculation tempts. I say no more of New Mexico as it is today, except that here surely is a place where many kinds of men live and work, where one may dig or dream, make poems, bricks or love, or merely sit in the sun, and find some tolerance and some companionship. Here handicraft as well as the machine has some place in life, the primitive persists beside the civilized, the changeless mountains offer refuge to the weary sons of change.

11

Revista Nueva Mexicana

LAWRENCE CLARK POWELL

Lawrence Clark Powell lives in Tucson, where he is professor in residence at the University of Arizona.

Seek essences, enduring things, touchstones, and symbols; try to re-create in prose what makes this country so increasingly meaningful and necessary to one. Altitude, distance, color, configuration, history, and culture—in them dwell the essential things, but they must be extracted. "Crack the rock if so you list, bring to light the amethyst." Costs nothing to try. Some have succeeded—Lummis, Lawrence, Long, La Farge, Horgan, Waters, the Fergussons—proving that it is possible. Stand books on the shelf, hang up maps, gaze in the turquoise ball, finger the fragment of red adobe from Pecos, reload the blue Scripto, take a fresh yellow pad, then sit down and see what comes.

Flying nonstop coast to coast, from 21,000 feet at 400 mph, one must look sharp and fast to determine landmarks. Oak Creek, Flagstaff, the sacred peaks of Coconino County, then the ammunition bunkers at Wingate, Gallup an absurdly small civilized scar, and Shiprock visible a hundred miles beyond; then Mt. Taylor, easternmost of the sacred Navajo peaks; and bearing northeast the Jemez range, the Rio Grande, Santa Fe hardly larger than Gallup, the Sangres and the dark blue of Taos Mountain, Eagle

Nest and Blue lakes, the red roofs of the Highlands University at Las Vegas; then excitement waning as the Middle West began, checkerboard earth, the three great rivers, Missouri, Mississippi, Ohio, and soon thereafter the sweeping descent to Idlewild. Ocean to ocean in seven hours, breakfast in Malibu, dinner in Manhattan, followed by humid days on the littoral, ameliorated by books and friends, meetings and talk, participated in by the mind earning a living, while the heart went on beating to Mountain Standard Time.

New York, Philadelphia, Pittsburgh, Chicago, Kansas City were heavy stopping stones to Albuquerque, as two planes conked out and four hours were lost. Dinner at last with Erna Fergusson in Old Town, as history and folklore, personal reminiscence and kindliness formed the aura of the town's First Lady, now living on a river ranch beneath a cathedral cottonwood.

The next night in Santa Fe I read aloud from Haniel Long's unfinished book and found it good, the ripe work of a writer who waited six decades to write his first novel. This was the fourth visit in two years to Haniel and Alice Long, and again I brought offerings of tea and affection and the feather of a dove; and faintly, very faintly, I envied him his twenty-year head start and his quintessential masterpiece, published in 1936, the *Interlinear to Cabeza de Vaca*.

At dinner on a high point east of town we looked across the river valley to Los Alamos, wickedly winking with lights, while a cottontail nibbled grass outside the window and the flares of sunset reached the zenith.

"You can't do both," Long said. "Lead the administrative life and write."

"I'm trying. And also I want to teach. It's taken me twenty years to learn librarianship. Now I want to teach it."

"I taught for two decades at Carnegie Tech before we came here. I like to think my books continue the process."

"It was your books that brought me here. The wide world's your classroom now."

And to illustrate this, Long gave me a German translation of the *Interlinear*, to add to the French one he gave me a year ago.

Burma born, Harvard schooled, tall, lean, and gray, and suffering the same eye trouble as Huxley's, this man who founded

Writers' Editions is humorous, quizzical, wise, and gentle, and I always leave him and his wife with a feeling of refreshment, redetermination, faith, and affection, and the anticipation of the riches which await a man in the decades between fifty and seventy, if he is prepared to recognize them.

"In youth the human body drew me and was the object of my secret and natural dreams. But body after body has taken away from me that sensual phosphorescence which my youth delighted in. Within me is no disturbing interplay now, but only the steady currents of adaptation and of sympathy." Thus speaks Long's conquistador.

The next day I entered the mission church at the Ranchos de Taos, one of the Southwest's two fairest shrines (the other being San Xavier). A party of nuns was being shown through by the priest, and they were having a jolly time, especially the youngest of the lot—a sister whose vitality, unquenched by her funereal habit, led her to peek under the red silk robe of an image to see what was beneath. I had not witnessed such spiritual vigor since Dublin.

Another memorable experience in Taos was the sight of a boy lying in the grass beside a watermelon truck parked by an *acequia,* reading a book, serious, intent, oblivious. When I passed again, hours later, the boy had turned from back to stomach and, propped on his elbow, was writing furiously, purposefully—what?

The sundrenched fields of Taos were lush with alfalfa, goldenrod, and dandelion, exuding midsummer fragrance to the point of asphyxiation. I had been reading *The Man Who Killed the Deer,* and I wanted to see the Blue Lake of the Taoseños. The sign promised a route, but it proved to be only by trail. The road corkscrewed fifteen miles up the Arroyo Hondo, down which white water was foaming. At Twining, elevation 9,412, the road became traversible only by jeep. The air was sharp, and smoke from a campfire rose unwaveringly into an eggshell sky. The bald dome of Mt. Wheeler rose another few thousand feet higher. A trail-sign pointed to Lobo Peak, on whose aspened shoulder I had visited Frieda Lawrence in 1941. An infestation of moths had stripped the aspens, and whole stands of them were shrouded with cocoons, while the filthy worms, known as the Great Basin tent caterpillar, fell in through the car windows.

Two uranium hunters were based here, a Texas father and son, with a Cadillac, a jeep, a scintillator, a forest service map, and a trailerload of grub. Father could have doubled for W. C. Fields. A sign read: "This is private property. You are welcome. Just mind your manners and don't pick the flowers."

The water of the western slope flows to the Rio Grande, and I followed it down the Arroyo Hondo through rocky junipered walls to its confluence with the Great River. The junction of watercourses is a good place to see the river-gods, and I sought to summon them by tossing stones into the bankside mud—the deep primeval ooze which acknowledged my offerings with a pluppity sound of thanks.

After supper I walked on a dirt road in the twilight, through a gate and into a field, with towering trees and Taos Mountain on one side and the Taos plain falling away on the other, clear to the Ranchos and the ranges beyond. I was rapt, remembering that four hundred years of history had passed by here, was quiet, hearing the whisper of ghosts around me, was content to be one link in an endless chain.

Everywhere I went the new edition of the New Mexico State Guide was open on the seat beside me, full of facts and photos and a minimum of misleading information. I never could find the church of San Miguel del Bado as described, or it must have been stuccoed over what the book said was stone, but the side-trip brought an even greater reward.

I had been earlier in Las Vegas, having come over the Sangres from Taos, through the Penitente villages of Picurís and Mora, traversing a high back country of few people and no people, of drizzle and shower and cloud-piled skies, past fields of corn and flowers and heavenly bluebirds, over the haunted route of Coronado, Armijo, and Los Tejanos, of Gregg and Kearny; and in the station there had seen mixed Santa Fe trains, none of which had quickened my pulse—cars, crews, passengers, all ordinary.

And then on this detour, having crossed the Pecos and reached the tiny station of Ribera, I saw a wondrous sight: the westbound Super Chief drawn up on a siding. That meant only one thing: its eastbound counterpart was due, and O Lord! there it was, coming round the turn, the long snake of silver Pullmans drawn by the monstrous red and yellow double diesel, pulling, pulling, with deep-throated, smoking exhausts, horning once for the passing, the engineer riding high on his throne, his gloved hand raised slightly in response to my enthusiastic wave, there at that orgasmic moment of midway meeting; and to crown it all, sight of an old friend, the Pullman car Coconino Princess, on which I had ridden before, coupled between Pine Meadow and Regal Junction, as fair a vision as these eyes have ever seen.

The westbound train gathered speed slowly and I lingered alongside it for several miles, its pony trucks clickety-clicking over the railpoints, until finally it pulled away from me, approaching Glorieta Pass and the descent to Las Vegas and Lamy. All through my lifetime, from the year of my birth, I had ridden over that same rail route, and now I knew that I would never ride that way again, preferring henceforth to go either by air or by auto. The engineer waved as I turned off to Pecos Pueblo, an ancient ruin abandoned in 1838 and now a state monument.

Rain began to fall again, darkening the red soil and the green piñons, and I got soaked while dashing in and out of the ruins of the church, which is dedicated to the same lady as my home town—Nuestra Señora la Reina de los Angeles. Without planning it I found myself traversing Pecos Village and once again following a river to its headwaters, while the car radio transmitted such sentimental songs as to make me long to learn the guitar—songs with apparently no other words than *corazon, amor, alma, y mujer*. Well, what else is there? *Libros.* I had not realized that this fabled river rises in the Sangres, and I preferred the mountain aspect of the stream, lined with a Cistercian monastery and a State Fish Hatchery and the strange modern hacienda of Arnold B. Friedman, to the lower Pecos country of Billy the Kid and worse.

This search for the source is a philosophical urge, as well as physiographical, a blind going upward to the beginning of things, while the world narrows in and all else is eliminated. This focus on the basic elements is purifying, therapeutic, electrifying, and this way of recharging by stripping away is a dedicatory one, well suited to this Angeleno who lives ordinarily in the midst of multiplicity. Such were my thoughts up where the Pecos rises.

The day's showers had been only a prelude to the storm I saw gathering overhead, and so I reluctantly wheeled around at the first possible point. It was the yard of a Justice of the Peace, who had thoughtfully provided his front porch with a bed, though sans mattress. A long way from the neoned wedding chapels of the Lower Sonoran. The cloudburst came as I regained Pecos Village, and the world disappeared behind a curtain of water, then just as quickly the clouds broke and the blueness of the sky made the eyes ache.

Sum it up. The spirit of religion, the sense of layered history, the enormous beauty of landscape under the blue and white sky and the starry darkness, a land of many-cultured richness lived in for at least a millennium and yet still sparsely peopled—these are some of the essences that northern New Mexico holds for me and which I find nowhere else on earth. Land of enchantment, land of nourishment, land of many good returns.

East of the Sandias the road runs north to Golden and Madrid. What's in a name? Much—especially if the name is foreign and musical. When asked for the most musical words in English, regardless of meaning, a foreigner replied "cellar door." Thus the Sandias, to one ignorant of Spanish. The Watermelon Mountains? Well, yes, as long as the mind doesn't visualize the seedy fruit.

The Sandia Mountains. Now different they appear when seen from the east, dark green and wooded all the way up, humped like a whale, without the bare face they present to Albuquerqueans. Southernmost of their sacred peaks, the range was called Turtle Mountain by the Pueblos. The turnoff to the crest was alluring, but I had miles to go before I parked, and the compass pointed north. Golden? Hardly. Madrid? A company coal town, obviously misnamed. The beauty of this lonely route lay in the piñon forest, and in the clouds that were beginning to cap the sky.

For it was another summer, and the daily thundershowers had begun. I was free of desk and phone and daily mail, and the people to whom must be given, if one wishes to get. I had gained New Mexico again with empty reservoirs, a week's prospect of pure isolation from the usual and a return home brimful of beauty.

At Cerrillos I came to an unexpected crossing of the railroad, the main line of the Santa Fe, and on a hunch I turned off and cruised through the village. I stopped by a group of natives on the porch of the grocery. "Any trains due?" I asked, briskly. Whereupon one of them lurched toward me, preceded by his boozy breath. "My friend," he pronounced, "there passes here one train every half hour," and he staggered back to his fellows. They laughed, as I drove on, crossed the tracks, and reconnoitered. Not a sound or sign of life, only shining rails. Then I spied a lank sack hanging from the trackside hook, and a car parked alongside, with a woman sleeping in it. The mail train was due. I waited, and pretty soon heard the low hum of an approaching diesel. A full five minutes passed before it burst round the curve, heading northeast to Lamy and Las Vegas, and bore down on the station with overriding urgency. The Super Chief, no less. The sack was hooked in, and an equally thin one thrown off. The silver vision passed. Toroweap, Tierra Amarilla, Cloudcroft, but this time my Princess was coupled elsewhere. The woman got out, picked up the sack, drove off. I had witnessed the postmistress of Cerrillos at work.

I paid my first visit to the Museum on the outskirts of Santa Fe, and saw an exhibition of contemporary arts and crafts of great beauty; silver and wood, turquoise and wool, the elements worked by hand with loving skill, the objects displayed in imaginative ways, to give one of the best museum experiences I have ever had.

City of the Holy Faith, huddle of abodes, cottonwooded, piñoned, ringed by ranges with ringing names: the Sangre de Cristos, the Sandias, the Jemez. Day's end and the mountains were blue black; again a lone rabbit, this time a big-eared jack, nibbling and sniffing his way across the somnolent landscape, as I looked north to the last light on Truchas, knowing that the morrow would find me on upland slopes.

The morrow was Sunday, and I saw people in their best, as once again I left the highway and took a dirt road to Chimayó and beyond, a gentle climb against the flow of water, past fields and flowers and burdened orchards. "Cherries, cherries," cried the children, from where they crouched by the roadside, holding out handfuls of the little red fruit.

All the beautiful choices were mine, whether to seek the fabled *santos* in the Santuario of Chimayó, or to see the Valley of Cordova, where Joseph Krumgold made *And Now Miguel,* that almost unbearably beautiful documentary film of sheepherding and a small boy's dream. One must always choose among several, and Truchas was my choice, an ancient village lying exposed on a hogback, inanimate on this Sunday morning, yet eternally alive, as the ghost towns of Arizona are not. Metals were not the reason for Truchas' naked site. The villagers built there originally for defense against their enemies, descending to the fields, or driving their sheep to mountain meadows.

I stopped and read in the guidebook: "In March 1772 an archive records the request of the villagers for twelve muskets and powder and protection from the Comanche. (Request denied). The walls of the adobe houses here are unusually thick (Truchas is a very cold place in winter). On a clear day are visible the La Plata Mountains 150 miles away in Southern Colorado; and Mt. Taylor, 150 miles south of west."

It was not *quite* that clear.

I crawled along the spinal street, seeing a crocheted peacock in a window, potted geraniums everywhere, a rainbow painted wall and matching eaves (someone was crazy for color), stacked woodpiles, and I breathed piñon smoke from cooking stoves.

At the general store I threaded a knot of black-garbed elders (no drunkenness here, but serious talk, of *agua* and *mujeres* and *caballos,* my ears told me) and browsed the merchandise, while drinking a 7-Up. Denim, gingham, leather, and straw were some of the staples my fingers felt, as I inhaled the dry-goods smell common to J. W. Robinson, Selfridge's, La Belle Jardinière, or wherever on earth.

Once again choice was necessary, and I bore north over piney slopes, instead of climbing higher toward the Truchas Peaks and the next highest point in New Mexico (Wheeler Peak, 13,151 feet; North Truchas Peak, 13,110 feet). I came at last to the *cor cordium* of Spanish New Mexico, the ancient village of Las Trampas. It was noon and the priest had locked the church and gone to lunch. So had everyone. The pueblo-like plaza was deserted, except for a car with Montana plates, but I could feel eyes on me, as I prowled around the classic church of Santo Tomás del Río de las Trampas, coming on a store of wooden crosses piled against the rear wall, evidence that this was indeed deep penitente country. At the front corner hung the only remaining bell, named *Gracia* because of its gentle tone—and this I verified with steady strokes of my strongest finger.

Leaving the village and descending toward Peñasco on the Rio Pueblo, I met a rodeo of pickup trucks and young men in white shirts, and a short distance beyond I saw a girl in a red dress disappearing through the piñons.

Entering Taos I got another sense of eternals from sight of my old watermelon truck, parked in the same place alongside the *acequia,* but honestly I cannot say the boy was reading. He must have finished the book and taken up something else.

And here, too, was the ubiquitous smell of burning piñon, recalling Peattie's words in his book on trees: "They say that those who, like Kit Carson, had once known the bells, the women and the pinyon smoke of Taos could never stay away—come Kiowa, come Sioux, come Kansas blizzard or calabozo."

El Crepusculo carried news of the death in San Diego of Bert Phillips, one of Taos' founding artists, and of the visit of Frieda Lawrence's daughter Barbara while Frieda's husband Angie was in Italy. I found Frieda in the house on the plain at El Prado, thanks to the directions of Joe Montoya's son at the family service station, where he was being aided by a swarm of boys, each of whom performed one automotive chore in slow motion, a pleasant change from metropolitan "minute men" service. I had not seen Frieda in five years, and found her still a fountain of friendly vitality. If Swift and Pope and the other bachelor misanthropes could have known a woman like Frieda, English literature would have been different, in the way it differed through what she gave Lawrence; and as we sat over tea and biscuits and spun the thread of talk clear back to the fateful day she first saw him in flannels and blazer and red beard, launching cockleshell boats for her children, I knew that this was basic to all literary history, that literature is made by men *and* women, a fact best understood by French critics.

South of Eagle Nest, State Highway 38 takes off to the east, giving promise, on the map, of a graded road over the mountains to Mora. The promise was not kept. What appeared on paper to be a beautiful back road was actually a deteriorating set of ruts, suited only to truck or jeep. I was driving a Chevrolet coupé, albeit a powerful eight-cylinder job, and with the automatic transmission which, contrary to popular belief, is excellent for slow driving over wretched roads, because of the uniform flow of power that can be maintained down to standstill and start again. And the car was high-bedded enough to clear the boulders; so it went, but just.

The road began alluringly enough along the adobe edges of sloping meadows. Still I had an eye on the sky. It was beginning to pile up with clouds that would break with rain before the day was ended, and I didn't want to be on dobe when they did.

There was no sign of life, even at the occasional ranches. The highway markers were rusted and illegible, and there was an increasing number of *trancas,* gated fences, requiring all my strength to manipulate. My eyes lifted to the blue mesa toward which the road climbed. Black Lake lay to the right, a natural *ciénaga* edged with deep grass and herds of fattening Herefords. This was the last place to turn back, but I did not know it, and pressed on ignorantly past the point of no return.

Suddenly the road narrowed and grew rockier. I drove at five miles an hour, grunting and sweating, in shorts and sneakers, thankful that my arms were stronger than my foresight, and really very happy not to be on Wilshire Boulevard. My comfort was a fresh set of tire tracks; otherwise I would not have known which choice to make when the road forked, as it did again and again.

Gaining the mesa at last I paused and looked back to the northernmost Sangres in the distance—Wheeler, Pueblo, and Lobos peaks, those bare "cloud-capp'd towers"—wondering how long I had before the rain came, and if there were *caliche* ahead, then turned my back on 'em and resumed my forward motion. The "road" rutted rockily through ponderosas and Engelmanns, then turned into a bouldered trough, down which I caromed toward what the map called Coyote Creek. It seemed to flow into the Guadalupita Valley, eventually to Mora and what, by contrast, would be civilization. This was the very opposite of the experience of seeking the headwaters of the Pecos and the Hondo: I longed to leave the headwaters, my muscles rigid under the hot flow of sweat, compelled to control my desire to hurry and beat the rain, and instead to crawl, bump, bounce, creep, and slither, holding horsepower and heartbeat in check. It had rained the day before, and the road was pooled and treacherous. And the flowers that bloom in the summer tra la got only sidelong looks from this scion of an old horticultural family. *¡Que lástima!*

Then the trough tossed me into a clearing—a sawmill, with promise of human beings, of whom I had not seen one since Eagle Nest three hours before. It was a big establishment, with many sheds and cabins and parked trucks, and piles of trimmings. But no saw buzzed. No voice spoke. There was no stock-pile of logs.

Nada. Nadie. Ninguno. En ninguna parte. The quintessence of nothingness. God, but it was eerie, like something out of Poe or Melville. I whistled. Echo answered. The tracks ended at still another fenced gate, leading to a ford over the creek. I parked and went around and faced a sign, and read, ABSOLUTELY NO TRESPASSING. Too late. I had already trespassed. Was this Highway 38, a public thoroughfare of the sovereign state of New Mexico, or was it a private road of the woodcutters? Had I taken a wrong turn up on the mesa?

And then I smelled and saw smoke, coming from a cabin chimney at the far end of the clearing. I trudged over spongy sawdust earth and called *Hola!* Two heads popped out of two windows, like boxed jacks, one red, one black. Grown boys, they belonged to, their mouths full of food, their eyes of astonishment.

"Where am I?" I asked. "Can I get out?"

They laughed and came outdoors. El Rojo was an Anglo, El Moro an *hijo de pais* who had stumps for hands.

"This is the sawmill of the Ortega Brothers," said Red, and Blackie added, "Where you from?"

"From Eagle Nest, Black Lake, and down the road to hell," I replied.

Again they laughed. "The worst is over," they assured me.

"Through the gate to Mora?"

"Sure, but don't be in a hurry. Those rocks are hungry."

"Where is everyone?" I asked.

"Logging. We just brought in a load and stopped for lunch."

"I have sweat the hunger out of me," I said.

"Where do you live?" they asked.

"In the City of Angels," I replied, "and I bring you blessings from Nuestra Señora."

They crossed themselves automatically, thinking perhaps I was a priest, garbed for a swim, and as I went back to my car, I heard them banging around in their cabin, whooping like Indians.

"The worst is over" was a way of speaking. The "road" forded and reforded Coyote Creek (a lovely stream under other conditions), shelving high along the bank on one side and then the other, rain-pooled, rocky, ribbon-narrow, dropping me fast with thunder at my back, and the only good omen a flight of blue birds across the very hood of the car.

The canyon kept widening, however, and the flow of sweat had slackened, my muscles relaxed, and I came at last to an angel—a woman in a white dress who vanished into her cabin as I drove up. In the window was the face of her daughter, who spoke sweetly in the grave manner of the country, when I asked her where I was.

"Guadalupita Valley," she said. "You bring rain with you. Gracias, señor."

"The road is better?"

"Truly a fine road hereafter."

"Thank you, thank you!" I said, as if she were personally responsible for this engineering miracle.

Shortly thereafter I turned off the road for a drive of cattle, headed for the high summer pastures, and I marveled at the working horses and their riders, Anglos all, with unfriendly eyes.

The rain caught up with me as I reached Guadalupita store and stopped to drink a cold bottle of soda pop, utterly relaxed as the fall turned to hail, then back to rain and finally to drip, cool on my hot skin. I snapped on the car radio and it crackled hopelessly with static.

At village edge I picked up a one-legged man, who raised a stick to stop me, and took him along my way to Mora. His name was Jesús Dorado, aged sixty-seven, bachelor, native of the valley, grower of pinto beans. Almost toothless, unshaven, dirty-overalled and smelly, Señor Dorado was essentially a gentleman, affable, informed as to the history and topography of the region, almost urbane, a representative spokesman for the land in his time. And he was amazed that I had come over that wild road in a city car.

The valley continued to widen as we neared Mora. West northwest the triple peaks of Truchas formed the horizon. Beyond

the eastern hills lay plains and rivers, the Ozarks, the Appala-
chians—pallid country, all of it. My compass swung west southwest.

I had not liked Mora on my first visit, and I liked it even less
this time, sensing there a focus of evil forces, personified by a
horseman leading another horse, an Anglo of such debauched
visage as to chill my blood.

Rolling down the road to Vegas I had an exciting glimpse of an
all but naked girl in a roadside *acequia,* and I thought of Frank
Waters' *People of the Valley,* laid in this very region, with its
beautiful episode of María and the soldier at the pool; and I was
uncertain as to which is the more memorable and lasting,
literature or life.

Another day I lunched with Waters at Los Alamos, where he
too serves the University of California, as information officer, and
I sensed no dichotomy between the man and his work, as is the
case in writers of lesser craft and character.

Flying back to Albuquerque in a Carco Beechcraft, I experienced
a feeling of flight not possible in a large plane. We blew off
The Hill's landing strip like a leaf in the wind, and floated out
over the valley of the Rio Grande, as the mesa fell away steeply
beneath us. I sat alongside the pilot, three other passengers in the
seat behind us, and he pointed out the pueblos as we passed over
them, following the serpentine source of life, matrix of New
Mexican history and culture, fed by snow and spring, the grand
configuration now visible in a glance, comprehensible in its
symbiotic parts, once seen all snowy frozen on a flight in winter,
then as a golden belt of cottonwoods in November, and now
green green, summer green, on this last river flight, under an
immensity of clouds which left shadows on the earth.

Rain and the Beechcraft fell together on the airport at Albuquerque, and I stood around on the edge of the cool curtain while
waiting for a westbound plane. Belted down in TWA's Flight 82,
then circling north over the city, I had a last sight of the Sandias
and a final good omen, not one but two perfect rainbows—*circo
iris, arcobaleno, arc-en-ciel, regenbogen, rainbow,* take your choice, all
beautiful, all blessed—arching from Bernalillo to where Highway
66 breached the range.

It was a turbulent flight, too rough to serve food and drink, and

I buckled down and read the society page of the *Santa Fe New Mexican,* able to absorb only the frothiest of prose.

Phoenix was hot, windy, sandy. I stayed belted in the plane.

Approaching the Colorado, we overtook the high brown front of the sandstorm, and then saw the river at Blythe, looped like silver on the dark body of earth, while the western sky gave the day angry ending, symbolic of the struggle between the states for the Southwest's most precious element. The land beneath me was California.

12

Hasta Mañana

MARY AUSTIN

Man is not himself only, not solely a variation of his racial type in the pattern of his immediate experience. He is all that he sees; all that flows to him from a thousand sources, half noted, or noted not at all except by some sense that lies too deep for naming. He is the land, the lift of its mountain lines, the reach of its valleys; his is the rhythm of its seasonal processions, the involution and variation of its vegetal patterns. If there is in the country of his abiding, no more than a single refluent color, such as the veiled green of sage-brush or the splendid wine of sunset spilled along the Sangre de Cristo, he takes it in and gives it forth again in directions and occasions least suspected by himself, as a manner, as music, as a prevailing tone of thought, as the line of his roof-tree, the pattern of his personal adornment.

Whatever this sense, always at work in man as the wheel is at work in the mill-race, taking up and turning into power the stuff of his sensory contacts, it works so deeply in him that often the only notice of its perpetual activity is a profound content in the presence of the thing it most works upon. He is aware of a steady purr in the midriff of his being, which, if he is an American, comes to the surface in such half articulate exhalations as "Gosh, but this a great country!"

To feel thus about your home-land is a sign that the mysterious quality of race is at work in you. For new races are not made new out of the dust as the first man was. They are made out of old races by reactions to new environment. Race is the pattern of established adjustments between the within and the without of man. Where two or three racial strains are run together, as coöperative adventurers in the new scene, or as conqueror grafting himself upon an earlier arrival, the land is the determining factor in the new design. By land, I mean all those things common to a given region: the flow of prevailing winds, the succession of vegetal cover, the legend of ancient life; and the scene, above everything the magnificently shaped and colored scene. Operating subtly below all other types of adjustive experience, these are the things most quickly and surely passed from generation to generation, marked, in the face of all the daunting or neglectful things a land can do to its human inhabitants, by that purr of inward content, the index of race beginning.

Here between the Rio Colorado and the Rio Grande, between the Colorado plateau and the deserts of Sonora and Chihuahua, it begins under such conditions as have always patterned the great cultures of the past, great, I mean, in their capacity to affect world culture and human history. In Greece, in Rome, in England, world power began with aboriginal cultures of sufficient rootage to have already given rise to adequate symbols, in art and social forms, of their assimilation to the land, upon which were engrafted later, invasive types, superior at least in their capacity to interrupt with determining force, the indigenous patterns. So, in our Southwest, we began with an aboriginal top-soil culture, rich in the florescence of assimilation, to which was added the overflow from the golden century of Spain, melting and mixing with the native strain to the point of producing a distinctive if not final pattern before it received its second contribution from the American East.

If I say that this American contribution is prevailingly Nordic, it is not because I commit myself to the swelling myth about a Nordic race, but because the term, for the moment, stands as the index of an accepted type. It is a type that, when its early representatives reached the land of its journey's ending across the incredible adventure of the Santa Fé Trail, was already established in a sense of race, a sense, at least, of reliance upon some deeply fleshed sinew of a common adaptive experience. It knew what it wanted, and moved instinctively by the shortest cuts to a generically Western accomplishment.

Your true man of race is always instinctive. It is only hybrids and the half-assimilated who rationalize and codify and suffer under the necessity of explaining themselves. For the first hundred years, not many Americans reached the Southwest who were not already partly assimilated to it, by their natures. It is, in fact, hardly three quarters of a century since the flag of American federation was raised in the plaza of Santa Fé. And already the land bites sharply into the deep self of the people who live upon it.